REGENTS RENAISSANCE DRAMA SERIES

General Editor: Cyrus Hoy
Advisory Editor: G. E. Bentley

THE WIDOW'S TEARS

GEORGE CHAPMAN

The Widow's Tears

Edited by

ETHEL M. SMEAK

UNIVERSITY OF NEBRASKA PRESS · LINCOLN

Regents Renaissance Drama Series

The purpose of the Regents Renaissance Drama Series is to provide soundly edited texts, in modern spelling, of the more significant plays of the Elizabethan, Jacobean, and Caroline theater. Each text in the series is based on a fresh collation of all sixteenth- and seventeenth-century editions. The textual notes, which appear above the line at the bottom of each page, record all substantive departures from the edition used as the copy-text. Variant substantive readings among sixteenth- and seventeenth-century editions are listed there as well. In cases where two or more of the old editions present widely divergent readings, a list of substantive variants in editions through the seventeenth century is given in an appendix. Editions after 1700 are referred to in the textual notes only when an emendation originating in some one of them is received into the text. Variants of accidentals (spelling, punctuation, capitalization) are not recorded in the notes. Contracted forms of characters' names are silently expanded in speech prefixes and stage directions, and, in the case of speech prefixes, are regularized. Additions to the stage directions of the copy-text are enclosed in brackets. Stage directions such as "within" or "aside" are enclosed in parentheses when they occur in the copy-text.

Spelling has been modernized along consciously conservative lines. "Murther" has become "murder," and "burthen," "burden," but within the limits of a modernized text, and with the following exceptions, the linguistic quality of the original has been carefully preserved. The variety of contracted forms (*'em, 'am, 'm, 'um, 'hem*) used in the drama of the period for the pronoun *them* are here regularly given as *'em*, and the alternation between *a'th'* and *o'th'* (for *on* or *of the*) is regularly reproduced as *o'th'*. The copy-text distinction between preterite endings in *-d* and *-ed* is preserved except where the elision of *e* occurs in the penultimate syllable; in such cases, the final syllable is contracted. Thus, where the old editions read "threat'ned," those of the present series read "threaten'd." Where, in the old editions, a contracted preterite in *-y'd* would yield *-i'd* in modern spelling (as in "try'd," "cry'd," "deny'd"), the word is here given in its full form (e.g., "tried," "cried," "denied").

Punctuation has been brought into accord with modern practices. The effort here has been to achieve a balance between the generally light pointing of the old editions, and a system of punctuation which, without overloading the text with exclamation marks, semicolons, and dashes, will make the often loosely flowing verse (and prose) of the original syntactically intelligible to the modern reader. Dashes are regularly used only to indicate interrupted speeches, or shifts of address within a single speech.

Explanatory notes, chiefly concerned with glossing obsolete words and phrases, are printed below the textual notes at the bottom of each page. References to stage directions in the notes follow the admirable system of the Revels editions, whereby stage directions are keyed, decimally, to the line of the text before or after which they occur. Thus, a note on 0.2 has reference to the second line of the stage direction at the beginning of the scene in question. A note on 115.1 has reference to the first line of the stage direction following line 115 of the text of the relevant scene.

CYRUS HOY

University of Rochester

Contents

Regents Renaissance Drama Series   v

List of Abbreviations   ix

Introduction   xi

THE WIDOW'S TEARS   1

Appendix: Chronology   111

List of Abbreviations

Brereton   J. Le Gay Brereton. "Notes on the Text of George Chap-
           man's Plays," *Modern Language Review*, III (1907), 62.
Chambers   E. K. Chambers. *The Elizabethan Stage*. Oxford, 1923.
Collier   J. P. Collier. *A Select Collection of Old Plays*. Vol. VI.
           London, 1825.
conj.   conjecture
corr.   corrected
Deighton   Kenneth Deighton. *The Old Dramatists: Conjectural
           Readings*. Westminster, 1896. Pp. 139–141.
Dodsley   Robert Dodsley. *A Select Collection of Old Plays*. Vol. IV.
           London, 1744.
Gifford   W. Gifford, ed. *The Plays of Philip Massinger*. New York,
           1860.
N & Q   *Notes and Queries*
OED   *Oxford English Dictionary*
Parrott   Thomas Marc Parrott, ed. *The Plays of George Chapman:
           The Comedies*. New York, 1961.
PMLA   *Publications of the Modern Language Association*
Q   Quarto, 1612
Reed   Isaac Reed. *A Select Collection of Old Plays*. Vol. VI.
           London, 1780.
S.D.   stage direction
Shepherd   R. H. Shepherd, ed. *The Works of George Chapman: Plays*.
           London, 1874.
S.P.   speech prefix
Tilley   Morris Palmer Tilley. *A Dictionary of the Proverbs in
           England in the Sixteenth and Seventeenth Centuries*. Ann
           Arbor, 1950.
uncorr.   uncorrected.

□   □

Introduction

DATE OF COMPOSITION AND STAGE HISTORY

The Widow's Tears, probably the last of Chapman's comedies, was published with the following title page:

The/ Widdovves Teares/ A/ Comedie./ As it was often presented in the blacke/ and white Friers./ *Written by* GEOR. CHAP./ [ornament]/ LONDON,/ Printed for *Iohn Browne,* and are to be sold at his shop/ in Fleet-street in Saint *Dunstanes* Church-yard./ 1612.

As is so often the case in the early seventeenth century, the date of publication is considerably later than that of composition. Charles W. Wallace dates the play prior to September, 1602,[1] but his evidence has been largely disproved. With the exception of Wallace, there is a general agreement among scholars that Chapman composed the play sometime in late 1605 or early 1606.[2] And, during the past thirty years, 1605 has been accepted by all scholars without hesitation. The evidence usually set forth, while not conclusive, is worthy of serious consideration and certainly fixes *The Widow's Tears* as a Jacobean rather than an Elizabethan drama. There is a reference to "strange knights" (IV.i.28), probably a satiric allusion to the number of knighthoods purchased from James I, and similar to two passages (I.i.263 ff.; IV.ii.77) in *Monsieur D'Olive* (1604–1605). There may also be a touch of satire in calling Rebus and his followers "Whoreson

[1] Charles W. Wallace, *The Children of the Chapel at Blackfriars, 1597–1603* (*The University Studies of the University of Nebraska,* no. VIII, 1908), pp. 82–168, *passim.*

[2] F. G. Fleay, *A Biographical Chronicle of the English Drama* (London, 1891), I, 61, states emphatically: "There is not a line in it which implies a later date than 1605." Felix E. Schelling, *Elizabethan Drama, 1558–1642* (Boston, 1908), I, 462, dates it *c.* 1605; E. E. Stoll, "On the Dates of Some of Chapman's Plays," *Modern Language Notes,* XX (1905), 208, between 1603 and 1605; T. M. Parrott, ed., *The Plays of George Chapman: The Comedies* (New York, 1961), p. 798, in the autumn of 1605 or spring of 1606.

bagpipe lords!" (I.ii.109), associating them with King James and his Scottish followers who flooded England after he was crowned king. Another piece of internal evidence concerns the reference to "monopolies," both in *The Widow's Tears* (I.i.118) and in *Monsieur D'Olive* (I.i.284). Although F. G. Fleay[3] feels that the statement in the former alludes to the Act of January, 1605, E. E. Stoll[4] points out that there is no such act under that date, but rather that in a proclamation of May 17, 1603, James I "called in" monopolies granted in the preceding reign. Thus the comedy must have been written after May, 1603. The satire on justice in the last act is probably an attack on the imprisonment of Chapman, Marston, and Jonson over the *Eastward Ho* affair in 1605.[5] T. M. Parrott believes that a date of 1605 "fits in well with the general chronology of Chapman's play," and that, in "tone and technic," *The Widow's Tears* indicates "a late period in his career as a writer of comedies."[6]

The comedy has not had a glorious stage history, although it may have been fairly popular during Chapman's day. In the dedication to Mr. Jo. Reed, the author speaks of "this poor comedy (of many desired to see printed)," and the title page alludes to the fact that "it was often presented in the blacke and white Friers." The play was acted at the Blackfriars by the Children of the Queen's Revels before they left that house toward the end of 1609 and was carried by them to their new quarters at Whitefriars. In the winter of 1612–1613, the group presented several plays at Court: Beaumont and Fletcher's *Coxcomb* (November, 1612) and *Cupid's Revenge* (January 1 and 9), and Chapman's *The Widow's Tears* (February 27, 1613). For the latter two plays Rossiter, the manager of the troupe, was paid £13 6s. 8d.[7] On January 12, 1668/9, Chapman's comedy was one of one hundred and eight plays, formerly acted at Blackfriars, allotted to Thomas Killigrew for performances at the Theatre Royal.[8] There is no record of its having been acted during or after the Restoration.

---

[3] Fleay, I, 61.

[4] Stoll, p. 208.

[5] *Ibid.*; Fleay, I, 61; Parrott, p. 798. E. K. Chambers in *The Elizabethan Stage* (Oxford, 1923), III, 257, argues that just at this time Chapman would avoid any further criticism of this kind.

[6] Parrott, p. 798.

[7] John Tucker Murray, *English Dramatic Companies, 1558–1642* (London, 1910), 364, n.; Chambers, II, 60.

[8] Allardyce Nicoll, *A History of Restoration Drama, 1660–1700* (2d ed.; Cambridge, 1928), pp. 315–316.

THE PLAY

The subject of *The Widow's Tears* is the inconstancy of women, especially of widows, who loudly protest their constancy to their husbands even after the latters' deaths. While many critics feel that Chapman's treatment of this theme is more cynical than need be, his tone and treatment are in keeping with the attitude toward women prevalent in the period. Chapman reflects the change in ethical mood from Elizabethan to Jacobean times, in which "satire supersedes moral suasion, and realism displaces romance."[9] Hardin Craig believes that Chapman

> may provide a solution to the riddle of woman's nature as the later dramatists [Webster, Middleton, and Ford] represent it. Chapman is pessimistic about the majority of women, whom his learning compelled him to believe were inferior to men in their powers of reason and were, by their very constitutions, bond to chance and wilfulness. Therefore, when Chapman develops his sympathy with or admiration for mere strength of passion, women come more and more into consideration. They have, he says, stronger souls than men, meaning that they are more prone to go to extremes in both good and evil.[10]

That men of the early seventeenth century saw a source of wit in the "wilfulness" of women, which often leads to infidelity, becomes clear through two different sources. First, jest books of the period make light of infidelity and poke fun at the swift remarriage of widows.[11] Second, the frailty of women is a dominant theme in Elizabethan and Jacobean drama. It is true that those, like Chapman, who wrote for the private theaters were far less likely to mince matters than those, like Shakespeare, who wrote for public playhouses. Alfred Harbage describes the main difference in attitude in this way:

> Although both bodies of drama [public and private] endorse chastity, only the popular plays are chaste. The others are "sexy"—in that they serve appetite and curiosity with erotic

[9] Hardin Craig, "Ethics in Jacobean Drama: The Case of George Chapman," *Essays in Dramatic Literature: The Parrott Presentation Volume* (Princeton, 1935), p. 28.

[10] *Ibid.*, p. 38.

[11] Marilyn L. Williamson, "Matter of More Mirth," *Renaissance Papers* (Columbia, S.C., 1956), p. 35.

stimuli, and reveal inadvertently the latitudes of conduct among leisured people for whom a cultivated sensuality has become an escape from boredom.[12]

The plays of the coterie which frequented the private houses "delight in cruel punishment and scenes of humiliation."[13] Further, as Harbage points out, "most of the jokes have to do with the inordinate sexual appetites of women, the sexual prowess or debility of men, the commercialization of sex especially through the use to which citizens put their wives, and sexual deviation."[14] While this is to some extent true of *The Widow's Tears*, it is equally true of the comedies of Jonson, Marston, and Middleton. Thus, Chapman's play is not at all unusual in its theme or in its treatment of women. The play is one of many which entertained the Jacobean London public with a representation of the age-old victory of the flesh and the world over weak human beings.

The Widow's Tears, like so many Elizabethan and Jacobean dramas, has two plots. Chapman does not intertwine them, but treats them consecutively. For the first three acts the emphasis is on the Tharsalio–Eudora subplot; the last two acts concentrate on the main plot, dealing with Lysander and Cynthia. The two plots are held together by common characters and by a common theme, with the subplot functioning almost as a unifying frame to the play as a whole.

In the subplot, the widowed Countess Eudora had vowed to her husband many times "in memory of him to preserve till death the unstain'd honor of a widow's bed" (I.i.84–86). But these vows are meaningless to Tharsalio. He is not a romantic young man. He frankly states that he has chosen to woo and win Eudora to gain wealth (I.i.42–44) and to restore the "decay'd" house of the Lysandri to its former eminence (III.i.47–48).

Tharsalio's courtship of Eudora takes place in three different scenes (I.ii., II.ii., and II.iv.), which develop the proposition that all women are susceptible to lusts of the flesh. Tharsalio—bold, witty, and confident—does his own courting in the first and third encounters. His brash approach is in sharp contrast to that of Eudora's other suitor, Rebus, who woos her with letters from his Altitude and with court gossip. He is a timid fellow who, although he resents Tharsalio's

[12] Alfred Harbage, *Shakespeare and the Rival Traditions* (New York, 1952), p. 190.
[13] *Ibid.*, p. 177.
[14] *Ibid.*, p. 221.

intrusion, attempts to hide his cowardice by invoking the honor of "the place." He and his companions, Psorabeus and Hiarbas, are not fully developed characters, nor should they be. They are mere shadows, and Tharsalio is the substance, the real thing. Set next to the dull Rebus, Tharsalio shines the more brilliantly.

Having made his first attack on "that fort of chastity," Tharsalio moves to the second step in his plan. He sends the "panderess" Arsace to Eudora to awaken the Countess's passion. As Arsace later says, "Never was man so prais'd with a dispraise, nor so spoken for in being rail'd on" (II.iii.2–4). Arsace's encounter with Eudora has aroused the ire of almost everyone who has written about *The Widow's Tears*. There is no question that the scene is a sensual one, but it is simply another example of the insistence on sex and eroticism in coterie drama. Further, the scene has thematic significance. It reinforces the portrayal of appearance versus reality on which the whole play hinges. Ostensibly Arsace has come to warn Eudora of the blemish to her honor, were she to wed Tharsalio; in reality she has come to advertise his incontinence and thus to arouse Eudora's lust. On the surface, Eudora is chaste, indignant at the mere idea that she might wed Tharsalio (or anyone else, for that matter), and disgusted by the bawdy innuendos voiced by Arsace; but it is all a pose, already seen through by Tharsalio, and now broken down by the procuress. Naught else remains but for her to forsake her vows of constancy, and this she does after her next encounter with Tharsalio. The third act ends with their marriage. Her function completed, Eudora drops out of the play until the very end, when, as is usual in Renaissance comedies, all the characters are present for the final resolution.

Samuel Schoenbaum compares the career of Eudora with that of Aurelia, the Duchess of Milan, in Middleton's *More Dissemblers Besides Women* (c. 1615). Both are widows who have pledged never to remarry; both are lauded for their virtue; both are finally betrayed by their awakened passion. "But there resemblance ends, for Chapman's portrayal of feminine weakness is unsoftened by the sympathetic awareness of human frailty that makes Middleton's duchess a moving, almost tragic figure."[15] The difference here, I think, is one of intention. In Middleton's play, when the Duchess learns that the man she loves, loves another, she gives up all claim to him and

<hr>

[15] Samuel Schoenbaum, "*The Widow's Tears* and the other Chapman," *Huntington Library Quarterly*, XXIII (August, 1960), 326.

embraces once again her vows of chastity. Clearly Middleton intends his moral to be overt; he intends that his chaste widow should remain chaste. Chapman, however, presents the frailty of women far more vigorously; his purpose is to show the discrepancy between high ideal and poor performance. Chapman's point is that Eudora and Cynthia are poseurs; that they, like most people in the world, cling to appearances, and that these appearances must be stripped from them. The difference finally is that Middleton's heroine is a strong woman and has been serious from the beginning about her vow (her seven years of constancy before her lapse testifies to this), while Cynthia and Eudora have so little self-knowledge that they fall easy prey to their emotions.

Cynthia's high ideal of herself is well displayed in her vehement reaction to the news of Eudora's betrothal to Tharsalio, and her comments serve to heighten the irony of her own fall later in the play. Her first reaction is one of horrified disbelief: "Is there probability in this, that a lady so great, so virtuous, standing on so high terms of honor, should so soon stoop?" (III.i.98–99). And indeed Eudora has stooped; she is betrothed to her former servant (though of good family), thus violating the principle of degree, just as Cynthia will when she stoops to "a base conjunction" for the love of an "eight-penny soldier." But even as Cynthia, in her pride and indignation, reaffirms her vow of chastity until death, her husband, stirred purposely to jealousy and suspicion of her widow's vows by Tharsalio, is hatching a plan to test her.

Thus, the first three acts are a prelude (admittedly a long one) to the major action of the play, laying the groundwork for the last two acts. Never for a moment have we been allowed to forget the subject of widow's constancy, and in Eudora's marriage to Tharsalio there is an indication of the fate of Cynthia, who will cast aside her vows much more quickly and eagerly than the Countess had done.

It has long been recognized that Chapman drew the Cynthia-Lysander plot from the *Satyricon* of Petronius. In Petronius, Eumolpus adds to his taunts concerning the fickleness of women by telling the story of a widow of Ephesus. This widow, despite the pleas of her relatives and friends, follows the body of her husband to the underground vault where she weeps night and day over his dead body. She and her maid, who has loyally followed her mistress, maintain their fast and vigil for five days and are highly lauded by all the city as a magnificent example of love and chastity. A soldier guarding the crucified bodies of some robbers in the graveyard is attracted by the light in the tomb and comes to investigate. Seeing the beautiful woman pining away for love, he entreats her to partake of food. The maid succumbs first to his entreaties and then persuades her mistress to eat and drink. The inevitable happens. After accepting food and drink, the widow also accepts the soldier's love, and they spend three nights enjoying their stolen pleasures. Their happiness, however, is brought to an end on the third night when the parents of one of the robbers, seeing the laxity of the guard, steal the body of their son. The soldier, terrified at the thought of the punishment he will receive, is about to commit suicide when the widow decides that they must put her husband's body on the cross. Eumolpus reports that "the soldier availed himself of this far-seeing woman's device, and the people wondered the next day by what means the dead man had ascended the cross." [16]

The bare outlines of Chapman's main plot are obviously here in Petronius, but Chapman has enlarged upon the details. Peter Ure points out that Chapman has turned Petronius' anecdote into "a full-dress Elizabethan comedy of manners with disguise, resurrection, male jealousy and female wit, and a quite fresh narrative pattern." [17] The whole affair hinges upon Lysander's feigned death to test his wife; the irony inherent in Petronius is increased in Chapman's play, for Cynthia mourns over an empty coffin. Further, it is the husband, disguised as a soldier, who tempts and wins his own wife, thus ironically proving that the widow's tears are false, even as he becomes his own cuckold. At this point, Chapman brings his two plots together through his manipulator, Tharsalio, who warns Cynthia and finally effects a kind of reconciliation between the husband and wife. Chapman's ironic contrasts and foreshadowings have actually increased the comic potential of Petronius' story.

Earlier critics, however, have not agreed that *The Widow's Tears* is a comedy in the conventional sense of the word. While they have granted its ironic power, they have often expressed horror over Chapman's treatment of the frailty of women in both plots. Paul V. Kreider would not apply the term "comic" either to the women or

16 Petronius Arbiter, *Satyricon*, cxii, trans. Michael Haseltine, Loeb Classical Library Edition (New York, 1903), p. 235.
17 Peter Ure, "The Widow of Ephesus: Some Reflections on an International Theme," *Durham University Journal*, XLIX, no. 1 (n.s. XVIII, no. 1, December, 1956), 4.

to the play. "The play is earnest. If not an authentic record of the playwright's observation of specific persons, Cynthia and Eudora are at least an unmistakable exploitation of a bitter theory concerning human nature." [18] Campbell focused his distaste on the Lysander-Cynthia plot when he wrote in *Lives of the Poets* that Chapman "has dramatized one of the most puerile and disgusting legends ever fabricated for the disparagement of female constancy." [19]

Those who have criticized the story of the Ephesian Widow and Chapman's use of it are forgetting that comedy basically arises from the inconsistency between human ideals and actual performance, or, one might say, from the frailty of mankind. Cyrus Hoy, who uses Petronius' anecdote as a point of departure for his discussion of comedy, tragedy, and tragicomedy, defines the essence of the tale, and of comedy in general, in these terms: "The irony of the reversal on which the story turns derives from the fine display of the incongruity of human intention and human deed which the Ephesian Widow's tergiversations afford; and incongruity is of the essence of comedy." [20]

Those who miss the joke and the irony of incongruity inherent in the tale of the Ephesian Widow and in Chapman's comedy are those who miss the essence of the play, which derives from the fact that most of the characters do not know themselves. They do not even know how to view the world. This appears most forcefully in the Machiavellian philosophy in the play. In some ways, *The Widow's Tears* seems to be one more of Chapman's experiments in the dramatic form—his attempt to give a valid portrayal of a Machiavellian character and a true interpretation of Machiavelli's philosophy as it can, and must, be applied to everyday life.

The belief, common in Renaissance England, that Italy was a place of vice and depravity, sin and evil, and that Machiavelli was a virtual incarnation of diabolical infamy, is well known. These beliefs were fostered by Roger Ascham in *The Scholemaster* (1570) and by Innocent Gentillet in his *Discourse . . . Against Nicholas Machiavell, The Florentine* (1576). Dramas of intrigue and political conniving were generally

[18] Paul V. Kreider, *Elizabethan Comic Character Conventions as Revealed in the Comedies of George Chapman* (Ann Arbor, 1935), p. 86.

[19] As quoted by S. Austin Allibone, *A Critical Dictionary of English Literature and British and American Authors* (Philadelphia, 1902), p. 368.

[20] Cyrus Hoy, *The Hyacinth Room: An Investigation into the Nature of Comedy, Tragedy, and Tragicomedy* (New York, 1964), p. 5.

located in Italy, and even when they were not, the villain of the piece was usually a Machiavellian character.

Although the Machiavellian was prominent in tragedy, he did not enjoy nearly such a vogue in comedy. Jonson's *Volpone* is set in Venice; Volpone himself, called the Fox, would doubtless bring to mind a Machiavel who sees and accepts man for what he is—greedy, vain, hypocritical—a man so knowledgeable about human nature that he can play on the weaknesses of man for his own good. And there are other comic villains as well—Barabas in Marlowe's *The Jew of Malta*, Malevole in Marston's bitter comedy *The Malcontent*, and, later, Luke in Massinger's *The City Madam*—all of whom are comparable to the treatment of the Machiavel in tragedy.

The Widow's Tears also shows the influence of Machiavellian ideas on English comedy. Interestingly enough, however, the play supports Machiavelli's theories. What Chapman does is to suggest that the contemporary attitude toward the corrupting influence of Italy is not really true; people are as they are, be they Italians, Italianate Englishmen, or whoever, and one must accept them as they are and forgive their frailties. Further, Chapman's Machiavellian character, Tharsalio, is not in the least typical of the usual stage presentation of the type.[21] He is, rather, a person who has learned to accept the world and its inhabitants for what they are. He is the spokesman for truth in the play, unpleasant as the truth sometimes is.

Early in Act I, Tharsalio is confident of winning the Countess Eudora, despite her vows. Cynthia, however, condescendingly attributes Tharsalio's attitude toward women not to wisdom, but to a diseased fancy:

> Brother, I fear me in your travel you have drunk too much of
> that Italian air, that hath infected the whole mass of your
> ingenuous nature, dried up in you all sap of generous disposition,
> poison'd the very essence of your soul, and so polluted your senses
> that whatsoever enters there takes from them contagion, and is
> to your fancy represented as foul and tainted, which in itself
> perhaps is spotless.   (I.i.125–131)

21 See Henry M. Weidner's "Homer and the Fallen World: Focus of Satire in George Chapman's *The Widow's Tears*," *Journal of English and Germanic Philology*, LXII (1963), 518–532, for an interpretation of Tharsalio as a Machiavellian malcontent and "lord of misrule." Weidner believes that it is Tharsalio who is "the chief object of satire" and who "stands for everything . . . Chapman denounces" (p. 519).

Cynthia's reference to Italian air is a reflection of the Gentillet-Ascham interpretation of Italy and of Machiavelli. In essence, she is sure that Tharsalio's visit to Italy has corrupted his sense of values.

Tharsalio's reply gives the other side of the Italy-Machiavelli issue, and it is this side that has most bearing on the play. "No, sister, it hath refin'd my senses, and made me see with clear eyes, and to judge of objects as they truly are, not as they seem, and through their mask to discern the true face of things" (I.i.132–135). Tharsalio echoes Machiavelli, who was concerned with showing things as they are and not as they seem, or as they are ideally conceived to be. The Florentine writes in Chapter XV of *The Prince* that "there is such a difference between the way men live and the way they ought to live, that anybody who abandons what is for what ought to be will learn something that will ruin rather than preserve him." [22] Later he states that "Everybody sees what you appear to be; few make out what you really are." [23] Machiavelli accepts man's weakness, his ingratitude, his ill will, as essentially a part of all human beings. Tharsalio, in his speech, emphasizes that he has a wisdom born of the ability to see beneath the appearance to the reality, to strip the mask from the face. As he continues his speech, he says that he can see "how short-liv'd widows' tears are, that their weeping is in truth but laughing under a mask, that they mourn in their gowns and laugh in their sleeves . . ." (I.i.135–137).

Cynthia had insinuated that Tharsalio was a victim of Italian influence. Yet, strikingly, it is she, Eudora, and Lysander who reveal more of the corruption and depravity voiced by Ascham and Gentillet. It is they who undergo a kind of metamorphosis, and not Tharsalio. Lysander sees Cynthia (and through her, all women) transformed before his very eyes from goddesslike purity to something akin to a devil. He asks himself:

> Is't possible there should be such a latitude in the sphere of this sex, to entertain such an extension of mischief and not turn devil? What is a woman? What are the worst when the best are so past naming? As men like this, let them try their wives again. Put women to the test; discover them; paint them, paint them ten

[22] Nicolo Machiavelli, *The Prince*, trans. and ed. Allen H. Gilbert (Chicago, 1946), p. 141.
[23] *Ibid.*, p. 150.

parts more than they do themselves, rather than look on them as they are; their wits are but painted that dislike their painting.

(V.i.218–226)

Lysander is a perfect example of the ruin which Machiavelli insists will come to one "who abandons what is for what ought to be." Cynthia pretends that she has known him all along and asserts that she is the

> Ill-destin'd wife of a transform'd monster,
> Who to assure himself of what he knew,
> Hath lost the shape of man!
>
> (V.i.479–481)

This imagery of transformation is also apparent in the conception of Eudora. She vehemently proclaims to Arsace that she abhors Tharsalio. But after Arsace's visit, she retires to herself, and her servants wonder if she is "not hatching some new monster" (II.iv. 38–39). In terms of her own misunderstanding of herself, she is, for she reverses all of her vows and opinions, and marries Tharsalio.

Of the four major characters, only Tharsalio is not associated with animal imagery. But this is as it should be. He is the only realist in the play, the one person who does not change, and the one person who has no illusions about himself, others, or the world.

It is Tharsalio, then, who sees beneath the exterior of all the characters. He never doubts for a moment that Eudora will forsake her vow and marry him. And as he has been right in his evaluation of Eudora, so is he correct in that of Cynthia. After having partaken of the soldier's food, Ero is ready to leave the tomb; she tells Cynthia that the "wonder's over, and 'twas only for that, that I endur'd this; and so, o' my conscience, did you" (IV.iii.32–33). But Cynthia is unable to maintain the world's illusion that she is a virtuous widow, for Tharsalio wakes her out of her "sleeping mummery," tells her the truth about the soldier, and warns her that there is no point in painting the tomb on the outside, for he is well aware of the "rotten carcasses" within. When Lysander dons his disguise once again for his last encounter with his wife, he, too, knows the difference between appearance and reality.

> Thou [disguise] that in truest shape hast let me see
> That which my truer self hath hid from me,
> Help me to take revenge on a disguise

Ten times more false and counterfeit than thou.
Thou, false in show, hast been most true to me;
The seeming true hath prov'd more false than thee.
(V.i.402–407)

But he is forgetting one thing: he is subject to whim and wilfulness;
he, too, is "false in show."

The very last action in the play—the scene of the imbecile Governor
and the resolution—has been condemned by all hands. Swinburne
felt that the "action of the last scene is again hampered by the
intrusion of forced and misplaced humours . . . [and] the story is
not so much wound up as huddled up in whispers and byplay. . . ."[24]
Kreider pointed out that the Governor is a stock figure of the "stupid
official" derived both from satire on English constables and the
Italian stage. He "monopolizes the stage in the last scene and prevents
the dramatist from developing the dénouement of a much better
action."[25] A. B. Whitmore was certain that the scene "mars the
play,"[26] while T. M. Parrott asserted that it "comes to an abrupt
and unsatisfactory close. . . . The solution is simply burked."[27]

Almost all readers would agree with these opinions. One probably
feels that the play is several pages too long because it reaches the
climax and the reversal when Cynthia walks out on Lysander. Yet
the play cannot end here, even though the action does. Parrott points
out that a reconciliation scene is missing,[28] but might not that have
turned the play from its highly satiric tone to a more sentimental one?
And that is exactly what Chapman chose to avoid. Instead, the
Governor, apparently a superfluous figure, comes on stage to grapple
blindly with justice and to "turn all topsy-turvy, and set up a new
discipline amongst you" (V.i.619–620). He has been unjustly
rewarded by Fortune, even as Argus is promoted in this scene for his
silly remarks and superficial knowledge. It is a mad world indeed
which the Governor proposes: utilizing an idea which appears

[24] Algernon C. Swinburne, "Essay on the Poetical and Dramatic Works
of George Chapman" from *The Works of George Chapman: Poems and Minor
Translations* (London, 1875), II, xxxi.

[25] Kreider, p. 103.

[26] Ada Blair Whitmore, "Chapman's Part in the Development of
Comedy" (unpublished Master's dissertation, The College of William and
Mary, 1935), p. 73.

[27] Parrott, pp. 802–803.

[28] *Ibid.*, p. 802.

frequently in Chapman, he would set up a discipline in which "no man shall do good but where there is no need" (V.i.631–632). His few sane statements are nullified by contradictory assertions. "I will whip lechery out o'th' city; there shall be no more cuckolds. They that heretofore were errant cornutos, shall now be honest shopkeepers, and justice shall take place. I will hunt jealousy out of my dominion" (V.i.634–638). Yet in his next speech, he contradicts the very basis of his reform: "It shall be the only note of love to the husband, to love the wife; and none shall be more kindly welcome to him than he that cuckolds him" (V.i.640–642). Further, he will "have all young widows spaded for marrying again" (V.i.648–649).

Aside from the thematic significance of the few speeches quoted above, the rescue of the innocent Lycus and the not-so-innocent Lysander from execution, the invitation to all to the wedding of Hylus and Laodice, and finally the joining of the hands of Lysander and Cynthia (none of which is executed by the brainless Governor), nothing in this final scene seems to have any bearing on the plot. It is my contention, however, that the scene has a valid structural and thematic function.[29]

The Governor is the epitome and the final summing up of the play. In such plays as *Bartholomew Fair*, *Volpone*, *Every Man in His Humor*, *Measure for Measure*, *The Great Duke of Florence*, *The City Madam*, and *The Fawn* (to name only a few), justice is effected by a valid figure of authority. But the Governor in *The Widow's Tears* is not one of these. This figure of justice is rather a fool, judging on the basis of appearance and caring nothing for the truth. At the end of the play, he is at a "non-plus"; nothing has worked out as he had anticipated, for both his criminals (who, by the way, only appeared to be guilty of the crimes of which they were accused) are vindicated. Further, the Governor serves as a surprise for those who expect, as everyone has a right to do, a more typically calm and judicious dénouement. But do not the Governor and the scene simply add one more comment to the theme of delusive appearances? He is not what he seems or what he should be, and neither is the world of the play. The first Soldier explains to his friend, who is horrified that Lycus may have killed Lysander: "Tush, man, in this topsy-turvy world, friendship and bosom kindness are but made covers for mischief, means to compass

29 Weidner, too, views the scene as "good satiric unraveling" (p. 530). However, his interpretation of the scene, as of the play and the character of Tharsalio, differs from the one set forth here.

ill. Near-allied trust is but a bridge for treason" (V.i.375–377). And that statement is a good description of the world of the play—a world in which Confidence wins over Chastity, in which faithful love turns to lust, in which a husband tests and tortures his wife to satisfy his own egotism. What could be a better summation of the comedy's theme than a character who is part and parcel of all that the play satirizes? And to make the conclusion further of a piece with all that has gone before, Tharsalio acts still as a sane, though cynical, chorus, even as he has done throughout the play. Appropriately, he has the last word as he tells Lysander to "think you have the only constant wife." The end of the play amounts to a wry demonstration of the truth of what Swift was to affirm a century later: that human happiness consists in a state of being continually well deceived.

THE TEXT

Since the 1612 Quarto of *The Widow's Tears* is the only seventeenth-century edition, it has complete authority. The comedy, along with *The Revenge of Bussy D'Ambois*, was entered on the Stationers' Register on April 17, 1612. The entry reads:

> Entred for his Copy vnder th' [h]andes of Sir George Buc[ke] and master warden Lownes, Twoo play bookes, ... vjd/ th' one called, *The Revenge of* BUSSY D'AMBOYS,/ beinge a tragedy,/ th[e] other called, *The wydowes teares*, being a Comedy, bothe written by George Chapman [30]

A single fee of sixpence was paid for both plays. Browne, who had published *May Day* in 1611 without obtaining a license,[31] entered the two plays on the Stationers' Register. *The Revenge of Bussy D'Ambois* was printed by T. S. (Thomas Snodham) for John Helme in 1613. However, W. W. Greg speculates that John Browne was the publisher of the tragedy, even though his name did not appear on the title page.[32] Certainly the Stationers' Register entry of February 17, 1623, which notes that Browne's widow transferred the rights of the tragedy to J. Marriot, would indicate that Browne held the rights to the play.

[30] Edward Arber, ed., *A Transcript of the Registers of the Company of Stationers of London, 1554–1640 A.D.* (New York, 1950), III, 218.

[31] W. W. Greg, *A Bibliography of the English Printed Drama to the Restoration* (London, 1939), no. 297.

[32] *Ibid.*, no. 307.

Greg does not record the transfer of rights by Browne or his widow for either *The Widow's Tears* or *May Day*. However, he does record a Stationers' Register entry on June 11, 1659, in which R. Marriot transferred both comedies to H. Moseley. The two plays were advertised in 1660 in Moseley's list, F 2, as no. 246 and no. 247 respectively.[33] It would seem that sometime between 1612 and 1659, Browne or his widow made a transfer of rights to Marriot, similar to the one recorded for *The Revenge of Bussy D'Ambois*. Marriot never printed any of these three plays. In fact, *The Widow's Tears* was not in print after the 1612 edition until Dodsley's *Select Collection of Old Plays*.

The external form of the copy-text is fairly clean. However, a number of alterations were made in the text while the sheets were passing through the press. Corrections, in substantives and accidentals, have been found in sheet B (outer forme), sheet C (inner and outer formes), sheet D (outer forme), sheet E (inner and outer formes), sheet K (inner forme), and sheet L (outer forme). In one respect the printing has presented the editor with one of her most formidable problems, that of distinguishing verse in passages printed as prose. While the Quarto prints obvious verse passages as prose all through the play, such passages occur far more frequently in Acts IV and V. Departures from the Quarto lineation in the present edition are indicated in the textual notes.

The exact nature of the printer's copy is not certain, although surmise is possible. The copy is certainly too clean for "foul" papers. The detailed stage directions on costuming, properties, action, and disguises, as well as the exits and entrances indicated, all point either to an authorial or to a stage version. Further, *Exiturus*, a rather unusual stage direction, and one distinctive of Chapman, is used four times in this play (see explanatory note to II.i.15). The play was probably printed from the author's holograph, which had been used as a theatrical prompt book. Parrott concurs in this conclusion.[34]

The printing of the 1612 Quarto was certainly endorsed by Chapman, as evidenced by his dedication to "Mr. Jo. Reed," in which he refers to the comedy, "(of many desired to see printed)." However, it is doubtful that the author oversaw the publication of the comedy. Chapman, had he checked the proofs, would easily have caught and objected to passages in which verse was printed as prose. In addition,

---

[33] *Ibid.*, no. 301 and no. 279.
[34] Parrott, p. 819, in note to V.ii.73–76.

there are a number of literals which the author would have insisted be corrected. As further evidence of compositorial, rather than authorial, revision is sheet D, on which there are five variants, all occurring in the outer forme. In the two appearing on sig. D1, Bodleian (Douce. C. 245) and Worcester College copies are obviously uncorrected. However, on D2^v and D3, they are the only two copies which have the -*a* rather than the -*o* spelling for *Sthenia*. I surmise that the compositor read Chapman's handwriting correctly, but that the proofreader, remembering the usual spelling in the text of the edition, had the *Sthenia* changed back to the -*o* form. For this reason, I have selected the "uncorrected" reading of *Sthenia* at II.ii.0.1 and II.ii.41.

The present edition is based on the collation of the following twenty-one copies of the 1612 Quarto: Bodleian Library (four copies); Boston Public Library; British Museum (three copies); Chapin Library; Dyce Collection, Victoria and Albert Museum (two copies); The Folger Shakespeare Library; Harvard University Library; Henry E. Huntington Library (two copies); Library of Congress; The Newberry Library; Pierpont Morgan Library; University of Texas Library; Worcester College; Yale Elizabethan Club.

ETHEL M. SMEAK

Mary Baldwin College

THE WIDOW'S TEARS

To the Right Virtuous and Truly Noble
Gentleman, MR. JO. REED,
of Mitton, in the County of Gloucester,
Esquire.

Sir, if any work of this nature be worth the presenting
to friends worthy and noble, I presume this will not want
much of that value. Other countrymen have thought the like
worthy of Dukes' and Princes' acceptations; *Gli ingiusti sdegni*,
Il pentimento amoroso, Calisto, Pastor fido, etc. (all being but   5
plays) were all dedicate to Princes of Italy. And therefore I
only discourse to show my love to your right virtuous and
noble disposition. This poor comedy (of many desired to see
printed) I thought not utterly unworthy that affectionate
design in me, well knowing that your free judgment weighs   10
nothing by the name, or form, or any vain estimation of the
vulgar; but will accept acceptable matter as well in plays as
in many less materials, masking in more serious titles. And
so, till some work more worthy I can select and perfect out
of my other studies, that may better express me, and more   15
fit the gravity of your ripe inclination, I rest,

Yours at all parts most truly affected,

GEO. CHAPMAN

4. *Gli*] *Parrott; not in Q.*   6. I] *Parrott; not in Q.*
5. *Calisto*] *Parrott; Calisthe Q.*

0.2. *Mr. Jo. Reed*]] plausibly identified by H. W. Crundell, "George
Chapman and the Grevilles," *N & Q*, CLXXXV and CLXXXIX
(August 28, 1943, and November 17, 1945), 137 and 213, as a relative of
Sir Fulke Greville.

0.3. *Mitton . . . Gloucester*] Mitton is not in the county of Gloucestershire,
but in Worcestershire, on the Gloucestershire border, near Tewkesbury
(Crundell).

4. *Gli . . . sdegni*] a pastoral drama by Bernardino Pino, published in
1553 and dedicated to Cesare Panfilio.

5. *Il . . . amoroso*] a pastoral drama written by Luigi Groto, the blind
poet of Adria, and dedicated to Vincenzo Naldi, Governor of Peschiera for
the Signoria of Venice, and to Marina Dolce Naldi, his wife (Parrott).

5. *Calisto*] a "nova favola pastorale" also by Groto, dedicated to Alfonso
II of Este, Grand Duke of Ferrara. It was first presented at Adria in 1561
and printed in 1583. See Walter W. Greg, *Pastoral Poetry and Pastoral
Drama, A Literary Inquiry* (London, 1906), pp. 442–443.

5. *Pastor fido*] Termed a "tragicomedia pastorale" by its author, Battista
Guarini, it was dedicated to Carlo Emanuele, Duke of Savoy, and published in 1590 (Greg, pp. 194–207).

THE ACTORS

THARSALIO, *the wooer*
LYSANDER, *his brother*
THE GOVERNOR *of Cyprus*
LYCUS, *servant to the widow Countess*
ARGUS, *gentleman usher* 5
[REBUS], *suitor to Eudora, the widow Countess*
TWO LORDS [PSORABEUS, HIARBAS, *followers of Rebus*]
HYLUS, *nephew to Tharsalio, and son to Lysander*
[CLINIAS, *servant to Eudora*]
CAPTAIN OF THE WATCH 10
TWO SOLDIERS
[GUARD]
EUDORA, *the widow Countess*
CYNTHIA, *wife to Lysander* 15
STHENIA, $\Big\}$ *gentlewomen attending on Eudora*
IANTHE,
ERO, *waiting-woman to Cynthia*
[LAODICE, *daughter to Eudora*
ARSACE, *a panderess*
TOMASIN, *a courtesan*] 20

3. THE GOVERNOR] *Parrott;* Thir. Gouernour *Q.*
4. LYCUS] *Dodsley;* Lycas *Q.,* but *elsewhere always* Lycus *in the quarto text.*
6–7. REBUS . . . *Rebus*] *this edn.;* 3. Lords suiters to Eudora the widdow Countesse *Q.*
9. CLINIAS . . . *Eudora*] *Parrott.*

12. GUARD] *this edn.*
15. STHENIA] *Dodsley;* Sthenio *Q.* *The "o" form appears throughout* Q *except at I.ii.36.3, where the "a" form appears, and at II.ii.0.1 and II.ii.41, where the "a" form appears in two copies of* Q.
18–20. LAODICE . . . *courtesan*] *Parrott.*

The Widow's Tears

A COMEDY

[I.i]   Tharsalio *solus, with a glass in his hand, making ready.*

THARSALIO.

    Thou blind imperfect goddess, that delights
    (Like a deep-reaching statesman) to converse
    Only with fools, jealous of knowing spirits,
    For fear their piercing judgments might discover
    Thy inward weakness and despise thy power,   5
    Contemn thee for a goddess; thou that lad'st
    Th' unworthy ass with gold, while worth and merit
    Serve thee for nought, weak Fortune, I renounce
    Thy vain dependence, and convert my duty
    And sacrifices of my sweetest thoughts   10
    To a more noble deity, sole friend to worth,
    And patroness of all good spirits, Confidence;
    She be my guide, and hers the praise of these
    My worthy undertakings.

    Enter Lysander *with a glass in his hand*; Cynthia, *Hylus, Ero.*

LYSANDER.

    Morrow, brother; not ready yet?   15

THARSALIO.

    No; I have somewhat of the brother in me. I dare say your
wife is many times ready, and you not up. Save you, sister;
how are you enamored of my presence? How like you my
aspect?

CYNTHIA.

    Faith, no worse than I did last week; the weather has   20

---

    12. *Confidence*] used here in the sense of "presumption," "audacious
assurance" (Parrott).

nothing chang'd the grain of your complexion.

THARSALIO.

A firm proof 'tis in grain, and so are not all complexions.
A good soldier's face, sister.

CYNTHIA.

Made to be worn under a beaver.

THARSALIO.

Ay, and 'twould show well enough under a mask, too.   25

LYSANDER.

So much for the face.

THARSALIO.

But is there no object in this suit to whet your tongue upon?

LYSANDER.

None, but Fortune send you well to wear it, for she best
knows how you got it.

THARSALIO.

Faith, 'tis the portion she bestows upon younger brothers,   30
valor and good clothes. Marry, if you ask how we come by
this new suit, I must take time to answer it; for as the ballad
says, "In written books I find it." Brother, these are the
blossoms of spirit, and I will have it said for my father's
honor, that some of his children were truly begotten.   35

LYSANDER.

Not all?

THARSALIO.

Shall I tell you, brother, that I know will rejoice you? My
former suits have been all spenders; this shall be a speeder.

LYSANDER.

A thing to be heartily wish'd; but, brother, take heed you

23. A ... sister] *Collier; Q prints as
separate line.*

21, 22. grain] In l. 21 *grain* means "quality" or texture; in l. 22 *in grain*
means "fast dyed" (Parrott).
24. *beaver*] a piece of armor, covering the lower part of the face.
32-33. *ballad ... it*] reference to unpaid accounts in tailor's books
(Parrott). The line was found frequently at the end of ballads and broadsides,
appealing to the gullibility of readers who believed that the ballad recounted
a true story because it was in print, according to Hyder E. Rollins, "The
Black-Letter Broadside Ballad," *PMLA*, XXXIV (1919), 330.

be not gull'd; be not too forward.   40

THARSALIO.

'T had been well for me if you had follow'd that counsel.
You were too forward when you stepp'd into the world
before me, and gull'd me of the land that my spirits and
parts were indeed born to.

CYNTHIA.

May we not have the blessing to know the aim of your   45
fortunes? What coast, for heaven's love?

THARSALIO.

Nay, 'tis a project of state. You may see the preparation, but
the design lies hidden in the breasts of the wise.

LYSANDER.

May we not know't?

THARSALIO.

Not unless you'll promise me to laugh at it, for without   50
your applause, I'll none.

LYSANDER.

The quality of it may be such as a laugh will not be ill
bestow'd upon't; pray heaven I call not Arsace sister.

CYNTHIA.

What? The panderess?

THARSALIO.

Know you (as who knows not) the exquisite lady of t
palace, the late governor's admired widow, the rich
haughty Countess Eudora? Were not she a jewel wor
wearing, if a man knew how to win her?

LYSANDER.

How's that? How's that?

THARSALIO.

Brother, there is a certain goddess called C
carries a main stroke in honorable prefe
waits upon her; Cupid is at her beck; she
errands. This deity doth promise me m
business.

57–58. *Were . . . her?*] proverbial (Tille
62–63. *of errands*] a common expressic

LYSANDER.

But if this deity should draw you up in a basket to your 65
countess's window, and there let you hang for all the wits in
the town to shoot at: how then?

THARSALIO.

If she do, let them shoot their bolts and spare not. I have a
little bird in a cage here that sings me better comfort. What
should be the bar? You'll say, I was page to the Count her 70
husband. What of that? I have thereby one foot in her favor
already. She has taken note of my spirit, and survey'd my
good parts, and the picture of them lives in her eye: which
sleep, I know, cannot close till she have embrac'd the
substance. 75

LYSANDER.

All this savors of the blind goddess you speak of.

THARSALIO.

Why should I despair but that Cupid hath one dart in store
for her great ladyship, as well as for any other huge lady
whom she hath made stoop gallant to kiss their worthy
followers? In a word, I am assured of my speed. Such fair 80
attempts led by a brave resolve are evermore seconded by
Fortune.

CYNTHIA.

But, brother, have I not heard you say your own ears have

65–67. *draw . . . at*] an allusion to a legend about Vergil current in the
Middle Ages. One version has it that Vergil's love for the daughter of the
Emperor of Rome is not returned, and to embarrass him she offers to
bring him secretly into her room by drawing him up in a box to her window.
The box stops in its course midway, and Vergil, suspended in full view of
the populace, affords great amusement to the Romans. In retribution he
causes all the fires in Rome to be extinguished; the only way they can be
rekindled is from the person of the Emperor's daughter. Tharsalio alludes
to the latter portion of the legend in I.ii.266–288. Domenico Comparetti
tells this tale in *Vergil in the Middle Ages*, trans. E. F. M. Benecke (London,
1895), pp. 326–327.

76. *blind goddess*] i.e., Confidence.

78. *huge*] great, in the sense of rank, power, or importance.

79. *she*] i.e., the blind goddess (l. 76).

79. *stoop gallant*] literally, dip (*stoop*) the flag (*gallant*), or salute. *OED*
[exp]lains the phrase as "something that humbles 'gallants'"; thus here it
[me]ans to "humble herself." See *stoop*, in the sense of "bow," in III.i.74.

been witness to her vows made solemnly to your late lord, in
memory of him to preserve till death the unstain'd honor of   85
a widow's bed? If nothing else, yet that might cool your confidence.

THARSALIO.

Tush, sister; suppose you should protest with solemn oath
(as perhaps you have done), if ever heaven hears your
prayers that you may live to see my brother nobly interred,   90
to feed only upon fish, and not endure the touch of flesh
during the wretched Lent of your miserable life; would you
believe it, brother?

LYSANDER.

I am therein most confident.

THARSALIO.

Indeed, you had better believe it than try it. But pray,   95
sister, tell me—you are a woman—do not you wives nod
your heads and smile one upon another when ye meet
abroad?

CYNTHIA.

Smile? Why so?

THARSALIO.

As who should say, "Are not we mad wenches, that can lead   100
our blind husbands thus by the noses?" Do you not brag
amongst yourselves how grossly you abuse their honest
credulities? How they adore you for saints, and you believe
it, while you adhorn their temples, and they believe it not?
How you vow widowhood in their lifetime, and they believe   105
you, when even in the sight of their breathless corse, ere they
be fully cold, you join embraces with his groom, or his
physician, and perhaps his poisoner; or at least, by the next
moon (if you can expect so long) solemnly plight new
hymeneal bonds with a wild, confident, untamed ruffian?   110

89. (as . . . done)] *Parrott; Q en-   *paren.*
closes ll. 89–90: (as . . . interred) *in*

100–101. *lead . . . noses*] proverbial (Tilley, N 233).
104. *adhorn*] reference to the horns of the cuckold.
108. *his poisoner*] "possibly a reference to *Hamlet*" (Parrott).
109. *expect*] await.

LYSANDER.

As for example?

THARSALIO.

And make him the top of his house and sovereign lord of the palace, as for example. Look you, brother, this glass is mine.

LYSANDER.

What of that?

THARSALIO.

While I am with it, it takes impression from my face; but 115 can I make it so mine, that it shall be of no use to any other? Will it not do his office to you or you, and as well to my groom as to myself? Brother, monopolies are cried down. Is it not madness for me to believe, when I have conquer'd that fort of chastity the great Countess, that if 120 another man of my making and mettle shall assault her, her eyes and ears should lose their function, her other parts their use, as if nature had made her all in vain, unless I only had stumbl'd into her quarters?

CYNTHIA.

Brother, I fear me in your travel you have drunk too much 125 of that Italian air, that hath infected the whole mass of your ingenuous nature, dried up in you all sap of generous disposition, poison'd the very essence of your soul, and so polluted your senses that whatsoever enters there takes from them contagion, and is to your fancy represented as foul and 130 tainted, which in itself perhaps is spotless.

THARSALIO.

No, sister, it hath refin'd my senses, and made me see with

125. travel] *Dodsley;* trauaile *Q*.

118–119. *monopolies . . . down*] Monopolies, the exclusive ownership or control of a public service by one party, had become a burden on the people during the latter part of Elizabeth's reign, and in a proclamation of November 25, 1601, she promised to "revoke all vexatious monopolies." But the reforms did not go through. Then, on May 7, 1603, her successor, James, "issued a proclamation bidding all persons to refrain from making use of their monopolies until they could satisfy the Council that they were not prejudicial to the interests of the nation." It is to this problem that Chapman alludes. Parrott gives the foregoing explanation in reference to *Monsieur D'Olive*, I.i.284–285.

126. *Italian air*] Cynthia refers to the anti-Italian, anti-Machiavellian feeling so prevalent in England during the early seventeenth century.

clear eyes, and to judge of objects as they truly are, not as
they seem, and through their mask to discern the true face
of things. It tells me how short-liv'd widows' tears are, that 135
their weeping is in truth but laughing under a mask, that
they mourn in their gowns and laugh in their sleeves; all
which I believe as a Delphian oracle, and am resolv'd to
burn in that faith. And in that resolution do I march to the
great lady.   140

LYSANDER.
You lose time, brother, in discourse. By this had you bore up
with the lady and clapp'd her aboard, for I know your
confidence will not dwell long in the service.

THARSALIO.
No, I will perform it in the conqueror's style. Your way is
not to win Penelope by suit, but by surprise. The castle's 145
carried by a sudden assault, that would perhaps sit out a
twelvemonth's siege. It would be a good breeding to my
young nephew here if he could procure a stand at the palace
to see with what alacrity I'll acoast her countessship, in what
garb I will woo her, with what facility I will win her.   150

LYSANDER.
It shall go hard, but we'll hear your entertainment for your
confidence sake.

THARSALIO.
And having won her, nephew, this sweet face,
Which all the city says is so like me,
Like me shall be preferr'd, for I will wed thee   155
To my great widow's daughter and sole heir,
The lovely spark, the bright Laodice.

LYSANDER.
A good pleasant dream.

THARSALIO.   In this eye I see
That fire that shall in me inflame the mother,
And that in this shall set on fire the daughter.   160

133–135. *to judge . . . things*] Tharsalio echoes Machiavelli; see Introduction, p. xx.
137. *laugh . . . sleeves*] proverbial (Tilley, S 535).
148. *a stand*] "a place of standing, position, station" (*OED*).
149. *acoast*] old form of "accost" (*OED*).

It goes, sir, in a blood; believe me, brother,
These destinies go ever in a blood.

LYSANDER.

These diseases do, brother; take heed of them.
Fare you well; take heed you be not baffl'd.

Exeunt Lysander, Cynthia, *Hylus, Ero. Manet* Tharsalio.

THARSALIO.

Now, thou that art the third blind deity   165
That governs earth in all her happiness,
The life of all endowments, Confidence,
Direct and prosper my intention.
Command thy servant deities, Love and Fortune,
To second my attempts for this great lady,   170
Whose page I lately was; that she, whose board
I might not sit at, I may board abed
And under bring, who bore so high her head.   *Exit.*

[I.ii]   [*Enter*] Lysander, Lycus.

LYCUS.

'Tis miraculous that you tell me, sir. He come to woo our
lady mistress for his wife?

LYSANDER.

'Tis a frenzy he is possess'd with, and will not be cur'd but
by some violent remedy. And you shall favor me so much to
make me a spectator of the scene. But is she, say you,   5
already accessible for suitors? I thought she would have
stood so stiffly on her widow vow that she would not endure
the sight of a suitor.

LYCUS.

Faith, sir, Penelope could not bar her gates against her
wooers, but she will still be mistress of herself. It is, as you 10
know, a certain itch in female blood: they love to be su'd to,
but she'll hearken to no suitors.

LYSANDER.

But by your leave, Lycus, Penelope is not so wise as her

161–162. *It . . . blood*] proverbial (Tilley, B 464). The phrase recurs at
I.ii.179; I.ii.188–189; II.iii.22–23.
164. *baffl'd*] disgraced.

husband Ulysses, for he, fearing the jaws of the siren, stopp'd his ears with wax against her voice. They that fear 15 the adder's sting will not come near her hissing. Is any suitor with her now?

LYCUS.

A Spartan lord, dating himself our great Viceroy's kinsman, and two or three other of his country lords, as spots in his train. He comes armed with his Altitude's letters in grace of 20 his person, with promise to make her a duchess if she embrace the match. This is no mean attraction to her high thoughts, but yet she disdains him.

LYSANDER.

And how then shall my brother presume of acceptance? Yet I hold it much more under her contentment to marry 25 such a nasty braggart, than under her honor to wed my brother: a gentleman (though I say't) more honorably descended than that lord, who, perhaps, for all his ancestry, would be much troubled to name you the place where his father was born.   30

LYCUS.

Nay, I hold no comparison betwixt your brother and him. And the venerean disease, to which they say he has been long wedded, shall I hope first rot him ere she endure the savor of his sulphurous breath. Well, her ladyship is at hand; y'are best take you to your stand.   35

LYSANDER.

Thanks, good friend Lycus.   [*Withdraws.*]

Enter Argus, *barehead, with whom another usher* Lycus *joins, going over the stage.* Hiarbas *and* Psorabeus *next,* Rebus *single before* Eudora, Laodice; Sthenia *bearing her train,* Ianthe *following.*

REBUS.

I admire, madam, you cannot love whom the Viceroy loves.

HIARBAS.

And one whose veins swell so with his blood, madam, as they do in his lordship.

36. S.D. *Withdraws*] *this edn.; Exit*
Q.

PSORABEUS.

A near and dear kinsman his lordship is to his Altitude   40
the Viceroy; in care of whose good speed here I know his
Altitude hath not slept a sound sleep since his departure.

EUDORA.

I thank Venus I have, ever since he came.

REBUS.

You sleep away your honor, madam, if you neglect me.

HIARBAS.

Neglect your lordship? That were a negligence no less than   45
disloyalty.

EUDORA.

I much doubt that, sir; it were rather a presumption to take
him, being of the blood viceroyal.

REBUS.

Not at all, being offered, madam.

EUDORA.

But offered ware is not so sweet, you know. They are the   50
graces of the Viceroy that woo me, not your lordship's, and
I conceive it should be neither honor nor pleasure to you
to be taken in for another man's favors.

REBUS.

Taken in, madam? You speak as I had no house to hide
my head in.   55

EUDORA.

I have heard so indeed, my lord, unless it be another man's.

REBUS.

You have heard untruth then. These lords can well witness
I can want no houses.

HIARBAS.

Nor palaces neither, my lord.

PSORABEUS.

Nor courts neither.   60

EUDORA.

Nor temples, I think, neither; I believe we shall have a god
of him.

---

50. *offered . . . sweet*] "a more elegant version of the proverb: *proferred
service stinketh*—Heywood's *Proverbs*, Pt. II, chap. 4" (Parrott).

Enter Tharsalio.

ARGUS.

See the bold fellow! Whither will you, sir?

THARSALIO.

Away! —All honor to you, madam!

EUDORA.

How now, base companion?   65

THARSALIO.

Base, madam? He's not base that fights as high as your lips.

EUDORA.

And does that beseem my servant?

THARSALIO.

Your court-servant, madam.

EUDORA.

One that waited on my board?

THARSALIO.

That was only a preparation to my weight on your bed,   70
madam.

EUDORA.

How dar'st thou come to me with such a thought?

THARSALIO.

Come to you, madam? I dare come to you at midnight, and
bid defiance to the proudest spirit that haunts these your
loved shadows, and would any way make terrible the access   75
of my love to you.

EUDORA.

Love me? Love my dog.

THARSALIO.

I am bound to that by the proverb, madam.

EUDORA.

Kennel without with him; intrude not here. What is it
thou presum'st on?   80

THARSALIO.

On your judgment, madam, to choose a man and not a

---

66. *fights*] in the sense of "contends" or "strives."
68. *court-servant*] possibly in the sense of *court*, to "woo," i.e., wooer,
courtier.
77. *Love me . . . dog*] proverbial (Tilley, D 496).

giant, as these are that come with titles and authority as they
would conquer or ravish you. But I come to you with the
liberal and ingenuous graces: love, youth, and gentry, which
(in no more deform'd a person than myself) deserve any   85
princess.

EUDORA.

In your saucy opinion, sir, and sirrah too; get gone, and
let this malapert humor return thee no more, for afore
heaven I'll have thee toss'd in blankets.

THARSALIO.

In blankets, madam? You must add your sheets, and you   90
must be the tosser.

REBUS.

Nay then, sir, y'are as gross as you are saucy.

THARSALIO.

And all one, sir, for I am neither.

REBUS [*drawing*].

Thou art both.

THARSALIO.

Thou liest; keep up your smiter, Lord Rebus.   95

HIARBAS.

Usest thou thus his Altitude's cousin?

REBUS.

The place, thou know'st, protects thee.

THARSALIO.

Tie up your valor then till another place turn me loose to
you. You are the lord (I take it) that wooed my great
mistress here with letters from his Altitude, which while   100
she was reading, your lordship (to entertain time) straddl'd
and scal'd your fingers, as you would show what an itching
desire you had to get betwixt her sheets.

HIARBAS.

'Slight, why does your lordship endure him?

82. giant] *Q* (*corr.*); By-but *Q*   94. S.D. *drawing*] *Parrott.*
(*uncorr.*).   101. straddl'd] *Dodsley;* strodl'd *Q*.

88. *malapert*] bold.

89. *toss'd in blankets*] a rough mode of punishment (*OED*).

97. *The . . . thee*] the location (i.e., the lady's presence) prohibits
violence.

REBUS.
>The place, the place, my lord.   105

THARSALIO.
>Be you his attorney, sir.

HIARBAS.
>What would you do, sir?

THARSALIO.
>Make thee leap out at window at which thou cam'st in.
>Whoreson bagpipe lords!

EUDORA.
>What rudeness is this?   110

THARSALIO.
>What tameness is it in you, madam, to stick at the discarding
>of such a suitor! A lean lord, dubb'd with the lard of others!
>A diseased lord, too, that opening certain magic characters
>in an unlawful book, up start as many aches in's bones as
>there are ouches in's skin? Send him, mistress, to the widow   115
>your tenant, the virtuous panderess Arsace. I perceive he has
>crowns in's purse that make him proud of a string; let her
>pluck the goose therefore, and her maids dress him.

PSORABEUS.
>Still, my lord, suffer him?

REBUS.
>The place, sir, believe it, the place.   120

THARSALIO.
>O, good Lord Rebus, the place is never like to be yours
>that you need respect it so much.

EUDORA.
>Thou wrong'st the noble gentleman.

THARSALIO.
>Noble gentleman? A tumor, an imposthume he is, madam;
>a very hautboy, a bagpipe, in whom there is nothing but   125
>wind, and that none of the sweetest neither.

---

108. *window . . . in*] a euphemism for an illegitimate birth.
109. *Whoreson bagpipe lords*] perhaps a hit at James and his Scottish lords.
Cf. l. 125: "a very hautboy, a bagpipe . . .."
115. *ouches*] tumors, carbuncles, or sores on the skin (*OED*).

EUDORA.

Quit the house of him by th' head and shoulders.

THARSALIO.

Thanks to your honor, madam, and my lord cousin the
Viceroy shall thank you.

REBUS.

So shall he indeed, sir.   130

LYCUS. ARGUS.

Will you be gone, sir?

THARSALIO.

Away, poor fellows.

EUDORA.

What is he made of? Or what devil sees
Your childish and effeminate spirits in him,
That thus ye shun him?—Free us of thy sight;   135
Be gone, or I protest thy life shall go.

THARSALIO.

Yet shall my ghost stay still, and haunt those beauties
And glories that have render'd it immortal.
But since I see your blood runs (for the time)
High, in that contradiction that foreruns   140
Truest agreements (like the elements
Fighting before they generate), and that time
Must be attended most in things most worth,
I leave your honor freely, and commend
That life you threaten, when you please, to be   145
Adventur'd in your service, so your honor
Require it likewise.

EUDORA.   Do not come again.

THARSALIO.

I'll come again, believe it, and again.   *Exit.*

EUDORA.

If he shall dare to come again, I charge you

127. shoulders] *Dodsley;* Soulders
Q.
133–136.] *Collier; Q prints* What . . .
him? *as prose, the remainder as verse:*

Free . . . sight;/ Be . . . goe.
137–138.] *Reed; prose in Q.*
149–150. If . . . him] *Parrott; prose
in Q.*

---

127. *Quit . . . shoulders*] variation of the proverbial, "To thrust out (in)
by the head and shoulders" (Tilley, H 274).

Shut doors upon him.

ARGUS.   You must shut them, madam,   150
To all men else then, if it please your honor,
For if that any enter, he'll be one.

EUDORA.
I hope, wise sir, a guard will keep him out.

ARGUS.
Afore heaven, not a guard, an't please your honor.

EUDORA.
Thou liest, base ass; one man enforce a guard?   155
I'll turn ye all away, by our isle's goddess,
If he but set a foot within my gates.

PSORABEUS.
Your honor shall do well to have him poison'd.

HIARBAS.
Or begg'd of your cousin, the Viceroy.   [*Exeunt.*]

                  Lysander [*comes forward*] *from his stand.*

LYSANDER.
This braving wooer hath the success expected; the favor I 160
obtain'd made me witness to the sport, and let his confidence
be sure, I'll give it him home. The news by this is blown
through the four quarters of the city. Alas, good confidence!
But the happiness is, he has a forehead of proof; the stain
shall never stick there, whatsoever his reproach be.   165

                  Enter Tharsalio.

What? In discourse?

THARSALIO [*aside*].
Hell and the Furies take this vile encounter!
Who would imagine this Saturnian peacock

158. S.P. PSORABEUS] *Parrott; Lurd.*   166.] *Q heads line with repetition of*
Q.   *speech prefix "Lysand."*
159. S.D. *Exeunt*] *this edn.; Exit Q.*   167. S.D. *aside*] *Parrott.*
159.1. *comes forward*] *this edn.*

---

156. *isle's*] Cyprus'.
165.1.] The action is continuous (Quarto has no scene division), but a
change of place is to be assumed.
168. *Saturnian peacock*] Saturnia was Juno, daughter of Saturn. Her
chariot was drawn by peacocks, birds traditionally associated with pride.

Could be so barbarous to use a spirit
Of my erection with such low respect? 170
'Fore heaven it cuts my gall; but I'll dissemble it.

LYSANDER.

What, my noble lord?

THARSALIO.

Well, sir, that may be yet, and means to be.

LYSANDER.

What means your lordship then to hang that head that hath
been so erected; it knocks, sir, at your bosom to come in and 175
hide itself.

THARSALIO.

Not a jot.

LYSANDER.

I hope by this time it needs fear no horns.

THARSALIO.

Well, sir, but yet that blessing runs not always in a blood.

LYSANDER.

What, blanketed? O the gods! Spurn'd out by grooms, 180
like a base bisogno? Thrust out by th' head and shoulders?

THARSALIO.

You do well, sir, to take your pleasure of me.   [*Aside.*]   I
may turn tables with you ere long.

LYSANDER.

What, has thy wit's fine engine taken cold? Art stuff'd in
th' head? Canst answer nothing? 185

THARSALIO.

Truth is, I like my entertainment the better that 'twas no
better.

LYSANDER.

Now the gods forbid that this opinion should run in a
blood.

THARSALIO.

Have not you heard this principle, "All things by strife 190
engender"?

170. erection . . . low] *Q* (*corr.*);   191. engender?] *Q* (*corr.*); engender
direction . . . loued *Q* (*uncorr.*).   *Q* (*uncorr.*).
182. S.D. *Aside*] *Parrott.*

---

181. *bisogno*] Italian word meaning a needy fellow or a raw recruit (*OED*).
190–192. *All . . . do*] proverbial (Tilley, T 166).

LYSANDER.

Dogs and cats do.

THARSALIO.

And men and women, too.

LYSANDER.

Well, brother, in earnest; you have now set your confidence
to school, from whence I hope't has brought home such a 195
lesson as will instruct his master never after to begin such
attempts as end in laughter.

THARSALIO.

Well, sir, you lesson my confidence still; I pray heavens your
confidence have not more shallow ground (for that I know)
than mine you reprehend so.   200

LYSANDER.

My confidence? In what?

THARSALIO.

May be you trust too much.

LYSANDER.

Wherein?

THARSALIO.

In human frailty.

LYSANDER.

Why, brother, know you ought that may impeach my 205
confidence, as this success may yours? Hath your observation
discovered any such frailty in my wife (for that is your aim
I know), then let me know it.

THARSALIO [aside.]

Good, good. —Nay, brother, I write no books of obser-
vations: let your confidence bear out itself, as mine shall me. 210

LYSANDER.

That's scarce a brother's speech. If there be ought wherein
your brother's good might any way be question'd, can you
conceal it from his bosom?

THARSALIO [aside].

So, so. —Nay, my saying was but general. I glanc'd at no
particular.   215

198. Well] Q (corr.); What Q   209. S.D. aside] this edn.
(uncorr.).   214. S.D. aside] this edn.

198. lesson] teach, instruct.

LYSANDER.

Then must I press you further. You spake (as to yourself,
but yet I overheard) as if you knew some disposition of
weakness where I most had fix'd my trust. I challenge you to
let me know what 'twas.

THARSALIO.

Brother, are you wise?   220

LYSANDER.

Why?

THARSALIO.

Be ignorant. Did you never hear of Actaeon?

LYSANDER.

What then?

THARSALIO.

Curiosity was his death. He could not be content to adore
Diana in her temple, but he must needs dog her to her   225
retir'd pleasures, and see her in her nakedness. Do you
enjoy the sole privilege of your wife's bed? Have you no
pretty Paris for your page? No young Adonis to front you
there?

LYSANDER.

I think none; I know not.   230

THARSALIO.

Know not still, brother. Ignorance and credulity are your
sole means to obtain that blessing. You see your greatest
clerks, your wisest politicians, are not that way fortunate;
your learned lawyers would lose a dozen poor men's causes
to gain a lease on't, but for a term. Your physician is jealous 235
of his. Your sages in general, by seeing too much, oversee
that happiness. Only your blockheadly tradesman, your
honest-meaning citizen, your not-headed country gentleman, your unapprehending stinkard, is blest with the sole
prerogative of his wife's chamber; for which he is yet 240
beholding, not to his stars, but to his ignorance. For if he be
wise, brother, I must tell you, the case alters. How do you
relish these things, brother?

228. young] Q (corr.); mysticall Q   242-243. How . . . brother?] Q
(uncorr.).   prints as separate line.

238. not-headed] "close cropped, in distinction from the long-haired
courtier" (Parrott).

LYSANDER.

Passing ill.

THARSALIO.

So do sick men solid meats. Hark you, brother, are you not 245
jealous?

LYSANDER.

No; do you know cause to make me?

THARSALIO.

Hold you there; did your wife never spice your broth with
a dram of sublimate? Hath she not yielded up the fort of
her honor to a staring soldado, and (taking courage from 250
her guilt) play'd open bankrout of all shame, and run the
country with him? Then bless your stars, bow your knees to
Juno. Look where she appears.

Enter Cynthia, Hylus [*and Ero*].

CYNTHIA.

We have sought you long, sir; there's a messenger within
hath brought you letters from the Court, and desires your 255
speech.

LYSANDER [*aside*].

I can discover nothing in her looks. —Go; I'll not be long.

CYNTHIA.

Sir, it is of weight, the bearer says; and besides, much hastens
his departure. Honorable brother! Cry mercy! What, in a
conqueror's style? But come and overcome?   260

THARSALIO.

A fresh course.

CYNTHIA.

Alas, you see of how slight metal widows' vows are made.

THARSALIO [*aside*].

And that shall you prove too ere long.

253.1 *and Ero*] Parrott.   263. S.D. *aside*] Parrott.
257. S.D. *aside*] Parrott.

---

249. *sublimate*] poison.   251. *bankrout*] bankrupt.
253. *Juno*] "referred to here as the protectress of marriage" (Parrott).
258–275.] The baiting of Tharsalio by Cynthia and Hylus has a counter-
part in Massinger's *Parliament of Love*, III.i., pp. 175–176 (Gifford), licensed
in 1624.
260. *come and overcome*] Anglicized proverbial form of Caesar's "veni,
vidi, vici" (Tilley, C 540).

CYNTHIA.

Yet for the honor of our sex, boast not abroad this your easy
conquest; another might perhaps have stay'd longer below   265
stairs. It but was your confidence that surpris'd her love.

HYLUS.

My uncle hath instructed me how to accost an honorable
lady; to win her, not by suit, but by surprise.

THARSALIO.

The whelp and all.

HYLUS.

Good uncle, let not your near honors change your manners;   270
be not forgetful of your promise to me, touching your lady's
daugher, Laodice. My fancy runs so upon't that I dream
every night of her.

THARSALIO.

A good chicken; go thy ways, thou hast done well; eat bread
with thy meat.   275

CYNTHIA.

Come, sir, will you in?

LYSANDER.

I'll follow you.

CYNTHIA.

I'll not stir a foot without you. I cannot satisfy the messenger's impatience.

LYSANDER.

(*He takes* Tharsalio *aside.*)   Will you not resolve me, brother?   280

THARSALIO.

Of what?

Lysander *stamps and goes out vex'd, with* Cynthia, Hylus, *Ero.*
So, there's veney for veney. I have given't him i'th' speeding
place for all his confidence. Well, out of this perhaps there
may be molded matter of more mirth than my baffling.
It shall go hard but I'll make my constant sister act as   285

---

266. It but was] *Q* (*corr.*); but   282–283. speeding place] *Q* (*corr.*);
vpon *Q* (*uncorr.*).   place speeding *Q* (*uncorr.*).

270. *let . . . manners*] proverbial (Tilley, H 583).
282. *veney for veney*] "tit for tat"; from a fencing term "venue," meaning
"thrust" (*OED*).
282–283. *speeding place*] the spot where a wound will be mortal.
284. *baffling*] see I.i.164, note.

famous a scene as Vergil did his mistress, who caus'd all the
fire in Rome to fail so that none could light a torch but at
her nose. Now forth! At this house dwells a virtuous dame,
sometimes of worthy fame, now like a decay'd merchant
turn'd broker, and retails refuse commodities for unthrifty 290
gallants. Her wit I must employ upon this business to prepare my next encounter, but in such a fashion as shall make
all split. Ho! Madam Arsace! —Pray heaven the oysterwives have not brought the news of my wooing hither
amongst their stale pilchards.   295

Enter Arsace, Tomasin.

ARSACE.

What? My lord of the palace?

THARSALIO.

Look you—

ARSACE.

Why, this was done like a beaten soldier.

THARSALIO.

Hark, I must speak with you. I have a share for you in this
rich adventure. You must be the ass charg'd with crowns 300
to make way to the fort, and I the conqueror to follow and
seize it. See'st thou this jewel?

ARSACE.

Is't come to that? Why, Tomasin.

TOMASIN.

Madam.

ARSACE.

Did not one of the Countess's serving men tell us that this 305
gentleman was sped?

TOMASIN.

That he did, and how her honor grac'd and entertained him
in very familiar manner.

286–288. *scene . . . nose*] see I.i.65–67, note.
292–293. *make all split*] the phrase has a nautical origin (Parrott); cf.
III.i.190, "till the vessel split again."
293–295. *oysterwives . . . pilchards*] Oysterwives, like ripiers (II.i.33),
were fish-peddlers and were apparently looked upon as gossips. A pilchard,
similar to a herring, is here associated with prostitutes.
298. *beaten*] experienced (*OED*).   306. *sped*] successful.

ARSACE.

And brought him down stairs herself.

TOMASIN.

Ay, forsooth, and commanded her men to bear him out of 310
doors.

THARSALIO.

'Slight, pelted with rotten eggs?

ARSACE.

Nay more, that he had already possess'd her sheets.

TOMASIN.

No indeed, mistress, 'twas her blankets.

THARSALIO.

Out, you young hedge sparrow; learn to tread afore you be 315
fledge.   *He kicks her out.*

Well, have you done now, lady?

ARSACE.

O, my sweet kilbuck.

THARSALIO.

You now, in your shallow pate, think this a disgrace to me;
such a disgrace as is a batter'd helmet on a soldier's head, 320
it doubles his resolution. Say, shall I use thee?

ARSACE.

Use me?

THARSALIO.

O holy reformation! How art thou fallen down from the
upper bodies of the church to the skirts of the city! Honesty
is stripp'd out of his true substance into verbal nicety. 325
Common sinners startle at common terms, and they that
by whole mountains swallow down the deeds of darkness,
a poor mote of a familiar word makes them turn up the
white o'th' eye. Thou art the lady's tenant.

ARSACE.

For term, sir.   330

THARSALIO.

A good induction; be successful for me, make me lord of
the palace, and thou shalt hold thy tenement to thee and

---

318. *kilbuck*] "a fierce-looking fellow" (*OED*).

thine heirs forever, in free smockage, as of the manner of
panderage, provided always—

ARSACE.

Nay, if you take me unprovided.   335

THARSALIO.

—Provided, I say, that thou mak'st thy repair to her
presently with a plot I will instruct thee in; and for thy surer
access to her greatness, thou shalt present her, as from thyself, with this jewel.

ARSACE.

So her old grudge stand not betwixt her and me.   340

THARSALIO.

Fear not that.
Presents are present cures for female grudges,
Make bad seem good; alter the case with judges.   [*Exeunt.*]

Finis Actus Primi.

[II.i]   [*Enter*] Lysander, Tharsalio.

LYSANDER.

So, now we are ourselves. Brother, that ill-relish'd speech
you let slip from your tongue hath taken so deep hold of my
thoughts, that they will never give me rest till I be resolv'd
what 'twas you said you know, touching my wife.

THARSALIO.

Tush, I am weary of this subject; I said not so.   5

LYSANDER.

By truth itself you did; I overheard you. Come, it shall
nothing move me, whatsoever it be. Pray thee unfold briefly
what you know.

THARSALIO.

Why briefly, brother, I know my sister to be the wonder of
the earth, and the envy of the heavens; virtuous, loyal, and   10
what not. Briefly, I know she hath vow'd that till death and

---

333. heirs] *Dodsley;* eares Q.   343. S.D. *Exeunt*] *this edn.; Exit* Q.

333. *smockage*] a nonce word from "socage," the tenure of land by the
performance of a service. "Smock" is usually suggestive of loose conduct
or immorality (*OED*).

after death she'll hold inviolate her bonds to you, and that
her black shall take no other hue, all which I firmly believe.
In brief, brother, I know her to be a woman. But you know,
brother, I have other irons on th'anvil.   *Exiturus.*   15

LYSANDER.

You shall not leave me so unsatisfied; tell me what 'tis you
know.

THARSALIO.

Why, brother, if you be sure of your wife's loyalty for term
of life, why should you be curious to search the almanacs
for aftertimes, whether some wand'ring Aeneas should   20
enjoy your reversion, or whether your true turtle would
sit mourning on a wither'd branch, till Atropos cut her
throat? Beware of curiosity, for who can resolve you?
You'll say, perhaps, her vow.

LYSANDER.

Perhaps I shall.   25

THARSALIO.

Tush, herself knows not what she shall do when she is transform'd into a widow. You are now a sober and staid gentleman. But if Diana for your curiosity should translate you into
a monkey, do you know what gambols you should play?
Your only way to be resolv'd is to die and make trial of her.   30

LYSANDER.

A dear experiment; then I must rise again to be resolv'd.

THARSALIO.

You shall not need. I can send you speedier advertisement

12–13. bonds . . . shall]   *Dodsley;*   13. firmly]   Q   *(corr.);*   firme   Q
bonds to you, & . . . shal Q *(corr.);*   *(uncorr.).*
bonds too, and . . . shall Q *(uncorr.).*

---

13. *black . . . hue*] proverbial (Tilley, A 436).
15. S.D. *Exiturus*] about to go. Chapman, who uses this stage direction
several times in this play, also employs it in *Bussy D'Ambois*, III.ii.323;
Conspiracy of Byron, II.i.96; *May Day*, II.i.130; and *Monsieur D'Olive*, V.ii.59.
20. *Aeneas*] a reference to Aeneas' affair with Dido.
21. *reversion*] "that which is left, i.e. the widow" (Parrott). *Reversion* is a
legal term, denoting "the right of succession to an office or place of emolu-
ment after the death or retirement of the holder" (*OED*).
28–29. *Diana . . . monkey*] For Diana's ability to turn men into beasts,
see also I.ii.222–226, a reference to her turning Actaeon into a stag.

of her constancy by the next ripier that rides that way with
mackerel. And so I leave you.   *Exit* Tharsalio.

LYSANDER.

All the Furies in hell attend thee; h'as given me   35
A bone to tire on with a pestilence. 'Slight, know?
What can he know? What can his eye observe
More than mine own, or the most piercing sight
That ever viewed her? By this light, I think
Her privat'st thought may dare the eye of heaven,   40
And challenge th'envious world to witness it.
I know him for a wild, corrupted youth,
Whom   profane ruffians, squires to bawds and strumpets,
Drunkards spew'd out of taverns into th' sinks
Of taphouses and stews, revolts from manhood,   45
Debauch'd perdus, have by their companies
Turn'd devil like themselves, and stuff'd his soul
With damn'd opinions and unhallowed thoughts
Of womanhood, of all humanity,
Nay, deity itself.

Enter Lycus.

Welcome, friend Lycus.   50

LYCUS.

Have you met with your capricious brother?

LYSANDER.

He parted hence but now.

LYCUS.

And has he yet resolv'd you of that point you brake with
me about?

LYSANDER.

Yes, he bids me die for further trial of her constancy.   55

35–36.] *Reed;* All . . . a/ Bone . . .
know? *Q*.

───────────────────────────

33. *ripier*] see I.ii.293–295, note.
34. *mackerel*] " a procurer or procuress" (*OED*).
36. *tire on*] a term of falconry, meaning to draw, pull, tug (*OED*).
46. *Debauch'd perdus*] "a morally abandoned person; a desperado; a
profligate, a roué." A *perdu* more often is used in the military sense of a
sentinel (*OED*).

LYCUS.

That were a strange physic for a jealous patient, to cure his
thirst with a draught of poison. Faith, sir, discharge your
thoughts on't; think 'twas but a buzz devis'd by him to set
your brains a-work and divert your eye from his disgrace.
The world hath written your wife in highest lines of honor'd   60
fame; her virtues so admir'd in this isle as the report thereof
sounds in foreign ears, and strangers oft arriving here (as
some rare sight) desire to view her presence, thereby to com-
pare the picture with the original.
Nor think he can turn so far rebel to his blood,   65
Or to the truth itself, to misconceive
Her spotless love and loyalty; perhaps,
Oft having heard you hold her faith so sacred,
As you being dead, no man might stir a spark
Of virtuous love in way of second bonds,   70
As if you at your death should carry with you
Both branch and root of all affection;
'T may be, in that point he's an infidel,
And thinks your confidence may over ween.

LYSANDER.

So think not I.   75

LYCUS.

Nor I, if ever any made it good.
I am resolv'd, of all, she'll prove no changeling.

LYSANDER.

Well, I must yet be further satisfied,
And vent this humor by some strain of wit.
Somewhat I'll do; but what, I know not yet.   *Exeunt.*   80

[II.ii]   *Enter* Sthenia, Ianthe.

STHENIA.

Passion of virginity, Ianthe, how shall we quit ourselves of
this panderess that is so importunate to speak with us?
Is she known to be a panderess?

65.] *Shepherd; prose in Q.*   [II.ii]
76.] *Shepherd;* I: . . . good. *Q.*   0.1.] *Sthenia Q (uncorr.); Sthenio Q
                                          (corr.).*

58. *buzz*] a false rumor.

IANTHE.

Ay, as well as we are known to be waiting-women.

STHENIA.

A shrew take your comparison.   5

IANTHE.

Let's call out Argus, that bold ass that never weighs what he
does or says, but walks and talks like one in a sleep, to relate
her attendance to my lady and present her.

STHENIA.

Who, an't please your honor? None so fit to set on any
dangerous exploit. Ho, Argus!   10

Enter Argus *bare.*

ARGUS.

What's the matter, wenches?

STHENIA.

You must tell my lady here's a gentlewoman call'd Arsace,
her honor's tenant, attends her to impart important business
to her.

ARGUS.

I will presently.   *Exit* Argus.   15

IANTHE.

Well, she has a welcome present to bear out her unwelcome
presence, and I never knew but a good gift would welcome
a bad person to the purest.—Arsace!

Enter Arsace.

ARSACE.

Ay, mistress.

STHENIA.

Give me your present; I'll do all I can to make way both for   20
it and yourself.

ARSACE.

You shall bind me to your service, lady.

STHENIA.

Stand unseen.

6. S.P. IANTHE] *Dodsley; Sthe. Q.*   10. Ho, Argus!] *Collier; Q prints as*
                                          separate line.

16. *bear out*] "support, back up" (Parrott).

-31-

Enter Lycus, Eudora, *Laodice;* Rebus, Hiarbas, Psorabeus *coming after;*
Argus *coming to* Eudora.

ARGUS.

    Here's a gentlewoman (an't please your honor), one of your
    tenants, desires access to you.   25

EUDORA.

    What tenant? What's her name?

ARGUS.

    Arsace, she says, madam.

EUDORA.

    Arsace? What, the bawd?   *She strikes* [*him*].

ARGUS.

    The bawd, madam? That's without my privity.

EUDORA.

    Out, ass; know'st not thou the panderess Arsace?   30

STHENIA.

    She presents your honor with this jewel.

EUDORA.

    This jewel! How came she by such a jewel? She has had great
    customers.

ARGUS.

    She had need, madam; she sits at a great rent.

EUDORA.

    Alas, for your great rent. I'll keep her jewel, and keep you   35
    her out, ye were best. Speak to me for a panderess?

ARGUS [*aside*].

    What shall we do?

STHENIA [*aside*].

    Go to; let us alone. —Arsace!

ARSACE.

    Ay, lady.

STHENIA.

    You must pardon us; we cannot obtain your access.   40

24–25.] *Collier;* Here's . . . (ant/   that's . . ..
Please . . . Honour) . . . Tennants/   28. S.D. *him*] *Parrott.*
Desires . . . you. *Q.*   37. S.D. *aside*] *Parrott.*
28. S.D.] *Parrott; Q prints S.D.*   38. S.D. *aside*] *Parrott.*
within l. 29: Madam? *shee strikes,*

---

    29. *privity*] knowledge.

ARSACE.

> Mistress Sthenia, tell her honor if I get not access to her, and
> that instantly, she's undone.

STHENIA.

> This is something of importance. —Madam, she swears your
> honor is undone if she speak not with you instantly.

EUDORA.

> Undone?   45

ARSACE.

> Pray her, for her honor's sake, to give me instant access to
> her.

STHENIA.

> She makes her business your honor, madam, and entreats,
> for the good of that, her instant speech with you.

EUDORA.

> How comes my honor in question? Bring her to me.   50

Arsace [*advances*].

ARSACE.

> Our Cyprian goddess save your good honor.

EUDORA.

> Stand you off, I pray. How dare you, mistress, importune
> access to me thus, considering the last warning I gave for
> your absence!

ARSACE.

> Because, madam, I have been mov'd by your honor's last   55
> most chaste admonition to leave the offensive life I led before.

EUDORA.

> Ay? Have you left it then?

ARSACE.

> Ay, I assure your honor, unless it be for the pleasure of two
> or three poor ladies that have prodigal knights to their
> husbands.   60

EUDORA.

> Out on thee, impudent.

ARSACE.

> Alas, madam, we would all be glad to live in our callings.

---

41. Sthenia] Q (*uncorr.*); *Sthenio* Q   50.1 *advances*] *Parrott; Enter Arsace*
(*corr.*).   Q.

EUDORA.

Is this the reform'd life thou talk'st on?

ARSACE.

I beseech your good honor, mistake me not; I boast of
nothing but my charity, that's the worst.   65

EUDORA.

You get these jewels with charity, no doubt. But what's the
point in which my honor stands endanger'd, I pray?

ARSACE.

In care of that, madam, I have presum'd to offend your
chaste eyes with my presence. Hearing it reported for truth
and generally that your honor will take to husband a young   70
gentleman of this city called Tharsalio—

EUDORA.

I take him to husband?

ARSACE.

If your honor does, you are utterly undone, for he's the most
incontinent and insatiate man of women that ever Venus
blest with ability to please them.   75

EUDORA.

Let him be the devil; I abhor his thought, and could I be
inform'd particularly of any of these slanderers of mine
honor, he should as dearly dare it as anything wherein his
life were endanger'd.

ARSACE.

Madam, the report of it is so strongly confident that I fear   80
the strong destiny of marriage is at work in it. But if it be,
madam, let your honor's known virtue resist and defy it for
him, for not a hundred will serve his one turn. I protest to
your honor, when (Venus pardon me) I wink'd at my
unmaidenly exercise, I have known nine in a night made   85
mad with his love.

EUDORA.

What tell'st thou me of his love? I tell thee I abhor him,
and destiny must have another mold for my thoughts than
nature or mine honor, and a witchcraft above both, to
transform me to another shape, as soon as to another conceit   90
of him.

90. conceit] *Collier;* conceipt *Q.*

ARSACE.

Then is your good honor just as I pray for you. And, good
madam, even for your virtue's sake and comfort of all your
dignities and possessions, fix your whole womanhood against
him. He will so enchant you as never man did woman; nay,   95
a goddess (say his light huswives) is not worthy of his
sweetness.

EUDORA.

Go to, be gone.

ARSACE.

Dear madam, your honor's most perfect admonitions have
brought me to such a hate of these imperfections that I   100
could not but attend you with my duty and urge his un-
reasonable manhood to the fill.

EUDORA.

Manhood, quoth you?

ARSACE.

Nay, beastlihood, I might say indeed, madam, but for
saving your honor. Nine in a night, said I?   105

EUDORA.

Go to, no more.

ARSACE.

No more, madam? That's enough, one would think.

EUDORA.

Well, be gone I bid thee.

ARSACE.

Alas, madam, your honor is the chief of our city, and to
whom shall I complain of these inchastities (being your   110
ladyship's reform'd tenant) but to you that are chastest?

EURODA.

I pray thee, go thy ways, and let me see this reformation
you pretend continued.

ARSACE.

I humbly thank your good honor, that was first cause of it.

EUDORA.

Here's a complaint as strange as my suitor.   115

_____

96. _light huswives_] loose women. Eudora echoes this phrase in
II.iv.245–246.

ARSACE.

I beseech your good honor, think upon him, make him an example.

EUDORA.

Yet again?

ARSACE.

All my duty to your excellence.   *Exit* Arsace.

EUDORA.

These sorts of licentious persons, when they are once re- 120
claim'd, are most vehement against licence. But it is the
course of the world to dispraise faults and use them, that so
we may use them the safer. What might a wise widow resolve
upon this point now? Contentment is the end of all worldly
beings. Beshrew her, would she had spared her news.   125
                                                           Exit.

REBUS.

See if she take not a contrary way to free herself of us.

HIARBAS.

You must complain to his Altitude.

PSORABEUS.

All this for trial is; you must endure
That will have wives, nought else with them is sure.   [*Exeunt.*]

[II.iii]   [*Enter*] Tharsalio, Arsace.

THARSALIO.

Hast thou been admitted then?

ARSACE.

Admitted? Ay, into her heart, I'll able it. Never was man
so prais'd with a dispraise, nor so spoken for in being rail'd
on. I'll give you my word, I have set her heart upon as
tickle a pin as the needle of a dial, that will never let it rest   5
till it be in the right position.

THARSALIO.

Why dost thou imagine this?

ARSACE.

Because I saw Cupid shoot in my words and open his

129. S.D. *Exeunt*] *Reed*; *Exit Q.*

---

2. *I'll able it*] "to *undertake*, or *answer for one*" (Reed).
5. *tickle*] unstable.

wounds in her looks. Her blood went and came of errands
betwixt her face and her heart; and these changes, I can   10
tell you, are shrewd telltales.

THARSALIO.

Thou speak'st like a doctress in thy faculty; but howsoever,
for all this foil, I'll retrieve the game once again. He's a
shallow gamester that for one displeasing cast gives up so fair
a game for lost.   15

ARSACE.

Well, 'twas a villainous invention of thine, and had a swift
operation; it took like sulphur. And yet this virtuous Countess hath to my ear spun out many a tedious lecture of pure
sister's thread against concupiscence; but ever with such
an affected zeal as my mind gave me she had a kind of secret   20
titillation to grace my poor house sometimes, but that she
fear'd a spice of the sciatica, which as you know ever runs in
the blood.

THARSALIO.

And as you know, soaks into the bones. But to say truth,
these angry heats that break out at the lips of these strait-   25
lac'd ladies are but as symptoms of a lustful fever that boils
within them. For wherefore rage wives at their husbands so,
when they fly out? For zeal against the sin?

ARSACE.

No, but because they did not purge that sin.

THARSALIO.

Th'art a notable siren, and I swear to thee if I prosper, not   30
only to give thee thy manor house gratis, but to marry thee
to some one knight or other, and bury thy trade in thy ladyship. Go, be gone.   *Exit* Arsace.

Enter Lycus.

THARSALIO.

What news, Lycus? Where's the lady?

LYCUS.

Retir'd into her orchard.   35

---

13. *retrieve the game*] "put up, or flush, the game a second time" (Parrott).
20. *gave me*] caused me to suspect.
21. *titillation*] desire.   22. *spice*] slight touch.
28. *fly out*] transgress (Parrott).

THARSALIO.

A pregnant badge of love, she's melancholy.

LYCUS.

'Tis with the sight of her Spartan wooer. But howsoever
'tis with her, you have practic'd strangely upon your brother.

THARSALIO.

Why so?

LYCUS.

You had almost lifted his wit off the hinges. That spark   40
jealousy, falling into his dry, melancholy brain, had well
near set the whole house on fire.

THARSALIO.

No matter, let it work; I did but pay him in's own coin.
'Sfoot, he plied me with such a volley of unseason'd scoffs as
would have made Patience itself turn ruffian, attiring itself in   45
wounds and blood. But is his humor better qualified then?

LYCUS.

Yes, but with a medicine ten parts more dangerous than
the sickness. You know how strange his dotage ever was on
his wife, taking special glory to have her love and loyalty to
him so renown'd abroad; to whom she oftentimes hath   50
vow'd constancy after life till her own death had brought,
forsooth, her widow-troth to bed. This he joy'd in strangely
and was therein of infallible belief, till your surmise began
to shake it; which hath loos'd it so, as now there's nought
can settle it but a trial, which he's resolv'd upon.   55

THARSALIO.

As how, man? As how?

LYCUS.

He is resolv'd to follow your advice, to die and make trial
of her stableness, and you must lend your hand to it.

THARSALIO.

What, to cut's throat?

LYCUS.

To forge a rumor of his death, to uphold it by circumstance,   60
maintain a public face of mourning, and all things apper-
taining.

41. brain] *Q* (*corr.*); braines *Q*   48. You know how] *Q* (*corr.*); how
(*uncorr.*).   know you *Q* (*uncorr.*).

46. *qualified*] calmed.

THARSALIO.

Ay, but the means, man? What time, what probability?

LYCUS.

Nay, I think he has not lick'd his whelp into full shape yet,
but you shall shortly hear on't.   65

THARSALIO.

And when shall this strange conception see light?

LYCUS.

Forthwith; there's nothing stays him but some odd business
of import which he must wind up, lest perhaps his absence
by occasion of his intended trial be prolonged above his
aims.   70

THARSALIO.

Thanks for this news, i'faith. This may perhaps prove
happy to my nephew. Truth is, I love my sister well and
must acknowledge her more than ordinary virtues. But
she hath so possess'd my brother's heart with vows and disa-
vowings, seal'd with oaths of second nuptials, as in that   75
confidence he hath invested her in all his state, the ancient
inheritance of our family, and left my nephew and the rest
to hang upon her pure devotion; so as he dead, and she
matching (as I am resolv'd she will) with some young prodi-
gal, what must ensue but her post-issue beggar'd, and our   80
house, already sinking, buried quick in ruin? But this trial
may remove it, and since 'tis come to this, mark but the issue,
Lycus; for all these solemn vows, if I do not make her
prove in the handling as weak as a wafer, say I lost my time
in travel. This resolution, then, has set his wits in joint   85
again; he's quiet?

LYCUS.

Yes, and talks of you again in the fairest manner, listens
after your speed—

THARSALIO.

Nay, he's passing kind, but I am glad of this trial, for all
that.   90

LYCUS.

—Which he thinks to be a flight beyond your wing.

85. travel] *Parrott;* trauaile *Q.*

---

64. *lick'd . . . shape*] proverbial (Tilley, S 284).
88. *speed*] success.

THARSALIO.

But he will change that thought ere long. My bird you saw
even now sings me good news and makes hopeful signs to
me.

LYCUS.

Somewhat can I say, too. Since your messenger's departure,   95
her ladyship hath been something alter'd, more pensive than
before, and took occasion to question of you, what your
addictions were, of what taste your humor was, of what cut
you wore your wit, and all this in a kind of disdainful scorn.

THARSALIO.

Good calendars, Lycus. Well, I'll pawn this jewel with thee,   100
my next encounter shall quite alter my brother's judgment.
Come, let's in; he shall commend it for a discreet and
honorable attempt.
Men's judgments sway on that side Fortune leans.
Thy wishes shall assist me.

LYCUS.   And my means.   *Exeunt.* 105

[II.iv]   [*Enter*] Argus, Clinias, Sthenia, Ianthe.

ARGUS.

I must confess I was ignorant what 'twas to court a lady
till now.

STHENIA.

And I pray you, what is it now?

ARGUS.

To court her, I perceive, is to woo her with letters from
Court, for so this Spartan lord's Court discipline teacheth.   5

STHENIA.

His lordship hath procur'd a new packet from his Altitude.

CLINIAS.

If he bring no better ware than letters in's packet, I shall
greatly doubt of his good speed.

IANTHE.

If his lordship did but know how gracious his aspect is to my
lady in this solitary humor.   10

---

92. *bird*] i.e., Arsace.
100. *calendars*] omens (Parrott).

CLINIAS.

Well, these retir'd walks of hers are not usual, and bode
some alteration in her thoughts. What may be the cause,
Sthenia?

STHENIA.

Nay, 'twould trouble Argus with his hundred eyes to descry
the cause.   15

IANTHE.

Venus keep her upright, that she fall not from the state of
her honor; my fear is that some of these serpentine suitors
will tempt her from her constant vow of widowhood.
If they do, good night to our good days.

STHENIA.

'Twere a sin to suspect her. I have been witness to so many   20
of her fearful protestations to our late lord against that
course; to her infinite oaths imprinted on his lips, and seal'd
in his heart with such imprecations to her bed, if ever it
should receive a second impression; to her open and often
detestations of that incestuous life (as she term'd it) of   25
widows' marriages, as being but a kind of lawful adultery,
like usury, permitted by the law, not approv'd; that to wed a
second was no better than to cuckold the first; that women
should entertain wedlock as one body, as one life, beyond
which there were no desire, no thought, no repentance from   30
it, no restitution to it. So as if the conscience of her vows
should not restrain her, yet the world's shame to break such a
constant resolution should repress any such motion in her.

ARGUS.

Well, for her vows, they are gone to heaven with her
husband; they bind not upon earth. And as for women's   35
resolutions, I must tell you, the planets, and (as Ptolemy
says) the winds have a great stroke in them. Trust not my
learning if her late strangeness and exorbitant solitude be
not hatching some new monster.

IANTHE.

Well applied, Argus; make you husbands monsters?   40

ARGUS.

I spoke of no husbands; but you wenches have the pregnant
wits to turn monsters into husbands, as you turn husbands
into monsters.

STHENIA.

Well, Ianthe, 'twere high time we made in to part our lady
and her Spartan wooer.   45

IANTHE.

We shall appear to her like the two fortunate stars in a
tempest, to save the shipwrack of her patience.

STHENIA.

Ay; and to him too, I believe, for by this time he hath
spent the last dram of his news.

ARGUS.

That is, of his wit.   50

STHENIA.

Just, good wittols.

IANTHE.

If not, and that my lady be not too deep in her new dumps,
we shall hear from his lordship what such a lord said of his
wife the first night he embrac'd her; to what gentleman such
a count was beholding for his fine children; what young   55
lady such an old count should marry; what revels, what
presentments are towards, and who penn'd the pegmas, and
so forth. And yet for all this, I know her harsh suitor hath
tir'd her to the uttermost scruple of her forbearance, and
will do more unless we two, like a pair of shears, cut asunder 60
the thread of his discourse.

STHENIA.

Well then, let's in. But, my masters, wait you on your
charge at your perils; see that you guard her approach from
any more intruders.

---

52. If . . . be] *Dodsley;* If not, &   55. fine] *Q* (*corr.*); fiue *Q* (*uncorr.*).
that my La: be *Q* (*corr.*); If not,   59. forbearance] *Q* (*corr.*); for-
that my Ladie be *Q* (*uncorr.*).   bearances *Q* (*uncorr.*).

---

46. *two fortunate stars*] "St. Elmo's fires, the electric phenomenon sometimes seen in storms at the mast-head or on the yard-arms of ships. In
ancient days this phenomenon was regarded as a manifestation of the Twin
Brethren, Castor and Pollux, stellified by Zeus, who were regarded as the
protectors of travellers by sea" (Parrott).

51. *wittols*] usually means a contented cuckold, but here it means a fool
or a person who has little sense. *OED* lists the latter meaning as a trans-
ference, "with a pun on *wit-all.*"

57. *penn'd the pegmas*] A *pegma* was originally a kind of framework or
stage, which sometimes bore an inscription, "hence *transf.* the inscription
itself." (*OED*).

IANTHE.

Excepting young Tharsalio.   65

STHENIA.

True, excepting him indeed, for a guard of men is not able
to keep him out, an't please your honor.

ARGUS.

O wenches, that's the property of true valor, to promise like
a pigmy and perform like a giant. If he come, I'll be sworn
I'll do my lady's commandment upon him.   70

IANTHE.

What, beat him out?

STHENIA.

If he should, Tharsalio would not take it ill at his hands,
for he does but his lady's commandment.

Enter Tharsalio.

ARGUS.

Well, by Hercules, he comes not here.

STHENIA.

By Venus, but he does; or else she hath heard my lady's   75
prayers and sent some gracious spirit in his likeness to fright
away that Spartan wooer that haunts her.

THARSALIO.

There stand her sentinels.

ARGUS.

'Slight, the ghost appears again.

THARSALIO.

Save ye, my quondam fellows in arms; save ye, my women.   80

STHENIA.

Your women, sir?

THARSALIO.

'Twill be so. What, no courtesies? No preparation of grace?
Observe me, I advise you, for your own sakes.

IANTHE.

For your own sake, I advise you to pack hence, lest your
impudent valor cost you dearer than you think.   85

CLINIAS.

What senseless boldness is this, Tharsalio?

68–69. like a pigmy] *Q* (*corr.*); like
Pigmey *Q* (*uncorr.*).

ARGUS.

Well said, Clinias, talk to him.

CLINIAS.

I wonder that notwithstanding the shame of your last
entertainment and threatenings of worse, you would yet
presume to trouble this place again.   90

THARSALIO.

Come, y'are a widgeon. Off with your hat, sir, acknowledge!
Forecast is better than labor. Are you squint-ey'd? Can you
not see afore you? A little foresight, I can tell you, might
stead you much, as the stars shine now.

CLINIAS.

'Tis well, sir, 'tis not for nothing your brother is asham'd on   95
you. But, sir, you must know we are charg'd to bar your
entrance.

THARSALIO.

But, whiffler, know you that whoso shall dare to execute
that charge, I'll be his executioner.

ARGUS.

By Jove, Clinias, methinks the gentleman speaks very   100
honorably.

THARSALIO.

Well, I see this house needs reformation. Here's a fellow
stands behind now, of a forwarder insight than ye all. What
place hast thou?

ARGUS.

What place you please, sir.   105

THARSALIO.

Law you, sir, here's a fellow to make a gentleman usher,
sir. I discharge you of the place, and do here invest
thee into his room. Make much of thy hair, thy wit will suit
it rarely. And for the full possession of thine office, come,
usher me to thy lady; and to keep thy hand supple, take   110
this from me.

95–96. on you] *Q* (*corr.*); in you *Q*
(*uncorr.*).

---

91. *widgeon*] a duck, whose proverbial stupidity is here associated with a
fool, or simpleton.

98. *whiffler*] one who clears the way for his master or for a procession.

ARGUS.

No bribes, sir, an't please your worship.

THARSALIO.

Go to, thou dost well. But pocket it for all that; it's no
impair to thee, the greatest do't.

ARGUS.

Sir, 'tis your love only that I respect; but since out of your 115
love you please to bestow it upon me, it were want of courtship in me to refuse it. I'll acquaint my lady with your
coming.   *Exit* Argus.

THARSALIO.

How say by this? Have not I made a fit choice, that hath
so soon attain'd the deepest mystery of his profession? Good 120
sooth, wenches, a few courtesies had not been cast away
upon your new lord.

STHENIA.

We'll believe that, when our lady has a new son of your
getting.

Enter Argus, Eudora, Rebus, Hiarbas, Psorabeus.

EUDORA.

What's the matter! Who's that, you say, is come?   125

ARGUS.

The bold gentleman, an't please your honor.

EUDORA.

Why, thou fleering ass, thou.

ARGUS.

An't please your honor—

EUDORA.

Did not I forbid his approach by all the charge and duty
of thy service?   130

THARSALIO.

Madam, this fellow only is intelligent, for he truly under-
stood your command according to the style of the Court of
Venus; that is, by contraries: when you forbid, you bid.

EUDORA.

By heaven, I'll discharge my house of ye all.

121. courtesies] *Dodsley;* courtsies
Q.

THARSALIO.

You shall not need, madam, for I have already cashier'd 135
your officious usher here, and choos'd this for his successor.

EUDORA.

O incredible boldness!

THARSALIO.

Madam, I come not to command your love with enforc'd
letters, nor to woo you with tedious stories of my pedigree,
as he who draws the thread of his descent from Leda's 140
distaff, when 'tis well known his grandsire cried cony skins in
Sparta.

REBUS.

Whom mean you, sir?

THARSALIO.

Sir, I name none but him who first shall name himself.

REBUS.

The place, sir, I tell you still, and this goddess's fair 145
presence, or else my reply should take a far other form
upon't.

THARSALIO.

If it should, sir, I would make your lordship an answer.

ARGUS.

Anser's Latin for a goose, an't please your honor.

EUDORA.

Well noted, gander, and what of that?   150

ARGUS.

Nothing, an't please your honor, but that he said he would
make his lordship an answer.

EUDORA.

Thus every fool mocks my poor suitor. Tell me, thou most
frontless of all men, did'st thou (when thou had'st means to
note me best) ever observe so base a temper in me as to 155
give any glance at stooping to my vassal—

THARSALIO.

Your drudge, madam, to do your drudgery.

136. choos'd] *Shepherd;* chos'd *Q.*

---

141. *cried cony skins*] peddled rabbits' skins.
149. *Anser's . . . goose*] Argus' Latin is correct.
154. *frontless*] shameless.

EUDORA.

—Or am I now so scant of worthy suitors that may advance
mine honor, advance my estate, strengthen my alliance (if I
list to wed) that I must stoop to make my foot my head? 160

THARSALIO.

No, but your side, to keep you warm abed. But, madam,
vouchsafe me your patience to that point's serious answer.
Though I confess, to get higher place in your graces I could
wish my fortunes more honorable, my person more gracious,
my mind more adorn'd with noble and heroical virtues; 165
yet, madam (that you think not your blood disparag'd by
mixture with mine), deign to know this: howsoever I once,
only for your love, disguis'd myself in the service of your late
lord and mine, yet my descent is as honorable as the proudest
of your Spartan attempters, who, by unknown quills or 170
conduits underground, draws his pedigree from Lycurgus his
great toe to the Viceroy's little finger, and from thence to
his own elbow, where it will never leave itching.

REBUS.

'Tis well, sir, presume still of the place.

THARSALIO.

'Sfoot, madam, am I the first great personage that hath 175
stoop'd to disguises for love? What think you of our country-
man Hercules, that for love put on Omphale's apron and sat
spinning amongst her wenches, while his mistress wore his
lion's skin and lamb-skinn'd him if he did not his business?

EUDORA.

Most fitly thou resembl'st thyself to that violent outlaw 180
that claim'd all other men's possessions as his own by his
mere valor. For what less hast thou done? Come into my
house, beat away these honorable persons—

180. outlaw] Q (corr.); Atlas Q
(uncorr.).

---

160. *stoop . . . head*] proverbial (Tilley, F 562).

171. *Lycurgus*] the famous Spartan lawgiver.

177–179. *Hercules . . . business*] Hercules was commanded by Apollo to
serve as a slave under Queen Omphale of Lydia for one year. During this
year he had to perform all kinds of female tasks for the Queen. Tharsalio
has cleverly twisted the legend for his own purposes.

179. *lamb-skinn'd*] "thrashed" (Parrott).

THARSALIO.

That I will, madam. Hence, ye Sparta-Velvets.

[*Beating them.*]

PSORABEUS.

Hold, she did not mean so.   185

THARSALIO.

Away, I say, or leave your lives, I protest, here.

HIARBAS.

Well, sir, his Altitude shall know you.

REBUS.

I'll do your errand, sir.   *Exeunt.*

THARSALIO.

Do, good cousin Altitude, and beg the reversion of the
next lady, for Dido has betroth'd her love to me. By this 190
fair hand, madam, a fair riddance of this Calydonian boar.

EUDORA.

O most prodigious audaciousness!

THARSALIO.

True, madam. O fie upon 'em, they are intolerable. And I
cannot but admire your singular virtue of patience, not
common in your sex, and must therefore carry with it some 195
rare endowment of other masculine and heroical virtues.
To hear a rude Spartan court so ingenuous a lady with dull
news from Athens or the Viceroy's Court, how many dogs
were spoil'd at the last bullbaiting, what ladies dubb'd
their husbands knights, and so forth.   200

EUDORA.

But hast thou no shame? No sense of what disdain I show'd
thee in my last entertainment, chasing thee from my
presence, and charging thy duty not to attempt the like
intrusion for thy life; and dar'st thou yet approach me in

184.1 *Beating them*] Parrott.

---

184. *Velvets*] wearer of velvet, a wealthy person; the term apparently
has a derogatory intent here. Cf. Beaumont and Fletcher, *The Scornful Lady*
(edn. 1616, sig. C1ᵛ), "my deare sparke of velvet."

189. *reversion*] see II.i.21, note.

191. *Calydonian boar*] the vicious boar which Artemis sent to ravage
the kingdom of Calydon because the people had neglected to offer a
sacrifice to her. The reference may be a double one here. The ancient name
of Scotland was Caledonia, and Chapman seems twice to have associated
this wooer with Scotland. See I.ii.109, note.

this unmannerly manner? No question this desperate bold- 205
ness cannot choose but go accompanied with other infinite
rudenesses.

THARSALIO.

Good madam, give not the child an unfit name; term it
not boldness which the sages call true confidence, founded
on the most infallible rock of a woman's constancy.   210

EUDORA.

If shame cannot restrain thee, tell me yet if any brainless
fool would have tempted the danger attending thy
approach.

THARSALIO.

No, madam, that proves I am no fool. Then had I been here
a fool, and a base, low-spirited Spartan, if for a lady's frown, 215
or a lord's threats, or for a guard of grooms, I should have
shrunk in the wetting and suffer'd such a delicious flower to
perish in the stalk, or to be savagely pluck'd by a profane
finger. No, madam, first let me be made a subject for
disgrace; let your remorseless guard seize on my despised 220
body, bind me hand and foot, and hurl me into your
ladyship's bed.

EUDORA.

O gods, I protest thou dost more and more make me admire
thee.

THARSALIO.

Madam, ignorance is the mother of admiration; know me 225
better, and you'll admire me less.

EUDORA.

What would'st thou have me know? What seeks thy coming?
Why dost thou haunt me thus?

THARSALIO.

Only, madam, that the Aetna of my sighs and Nilus of my
tears, pour'd forth in your presence, might witness to your 230
honor the hot and moist affection of my heart, and work me
some measure of favor from your sweet tongue, or your
sweeter lips, or what else your good ladyship shall esteem
more conducible to your divine contentment.

217. *shrunk in the wetting*] been put to the test and found lacking.
226. *admire*] wonder at.

EUDORA.

Pen and ink-horn, I thank thee. This you learn'd when you 235
were a servingman.

THARSALIO.

Madam, I am still the same creature, and I will so tie my
whole fortunes to that style, as were it my happiness (as I
know it will be) to mount into my lord's succession, yet vow I
never to assume other title or state than your servant's; not 240
approaching your board, but bidden; not pressing to your
bed, but your pleasure shall be first known if you will
command me any service.

EUDORA.

Thy vows are as vain as a ruffian's oaths, as common as the
air, and as cheap as the dust. How many of the light 245
huswives, thy muses, hath thy love promis'd this service
besides, I pray thee?

THARSALIO.

Compare shadows to bodies, madam, pictures to the life,
and such are they to you, in my valuation.

EUDORA.

I see words will never free me of thy boldness, and will 250
therefore now use blows, and those of the mortalest enforce-
ment. Let it suffice, sir, that all this time, and to this place,
you enjoy your safety. Keep back, no one foot follow me
further; for I protest to thee, the next threshold pass'd,
lets pass a prepar'd ambush to thy latest breath.   255

Exit Eudora.

THARSALIO.

This for your ambush.   (*He draws.*)   Dare my love with
death?   [*Exit.*]

CLINIAS.

'Slight, follow, an't please your honor.

ARGUS.

Not I, by this light.

240. servant's] *conj. Brereton, accep-*   254. pass'd] *this edn.;* past *Q.*
ted Parrott; seruants *Q.*

235. *ink-horn*] i.e., ink-horn terms, with reference to the bookish language
of Tharsalio's preceding speech.

CLINIAS.

I hope, gentlewomen, you will.   260

STHENIA.

Not we, sir; we are no parters of frays.

CLINIAS.

Faith, nor I'll be any breaker of customs.   *Exeunt.*

Finis Actus Secundi.

[III.i]   *Enter* Lysander *and* Lycus, *booted.*

LYCUS.

Would any heart of adamant, for satisfaction of an un-
grounded humor, rack a poor lady's innocency as you intend
to do? It was a strange curiosity in that Emperor, that
ripp'd his mother's womb to see the place he lay in.

LYSANDER.

Come, do not load me with volumes of persuasion; I am   5
resolv'd, if she be gold she may abide the tast. Let's away.
I wonder where this wild brother is.

Enter Cynthia, Hylus, *and* Ero.

CYNTHIA.

Sir—

LYSANDER.

I pray thee, wife, show but thyself a woman, and be silent.
Question no more the reason of my journey, which our great   10
Viceroy's charge, urg'd in this letter, doth enforce me to.

CYNTHIA.

Let me but see that letter; there is something
In this presaging blood of mine tells me
This sudden journey can portend no good.
Resolve me, sweet; have not I given you cause   15
Of discontent by some misprision,

12–18.] *Parrott; prose in Q.*

3–4. *It was . . . he lay in*] "This seems to be an exaggerated form of the
report preserved in *Suetonius* (Nero, 34) that Nero inspected the body of the
mother he had murdered, handled it, praised and blamed her figure, and
so on" (Parrott).
6. *tast*] an old form of "taste" in the sense of "touch" or "test" (*OED*).
16. *misprision*] omission or misunderstanding (*OED*).

Or want of fit observance? Let me know,
That I may wreak myself upon myself.

LYSANDER.

Come, wife, our love is now grown old and staid,
And must not wanton it in tricks of court,   20
Nor interchang'd delights of melting lovers,
Hanging on sleeves, sighing, loath to depart.
These toys are past with us; our true love's substance
Hath worn out all the show. Let it suffice
I hold thee dear; and think some cause of weight,   25
With no excuse to be dispens'd withal,
Compels me from thy most desir'd embraces.
I stay but for my brother; came he not in last night?

HYLUS.

For certain no, sir, which gave us cause of wonder what
accident kept him abroad.   30

CYNTHIA.

Pray heaven it prove not some wild resolution bred in him by
his second repulse from the Countess.

LYSANDER.

Trust me, I something fear it. This insatiate spirit of aspiring,
being so dangerous and fatal, desire mounted on the wings
of it, descends not but headlong.   35

HYLUS.

Sir, sir, here's my uncle.

Enter Tharsalio [*cloaked*].

LYSANDER.

What, wrapp'd in careless cloak, face hid in hat unbanded?
These are the ditches, brother, in which outraging colts
plunge both themselves and their riders.

THARSALIO.

Well, we must get out as well as we may; if not, there's the   40
making of a grave sav'd.

CYNTHIA.

That's desperately spoken, brother; had it not been happier
the colt had been better broken, and his rider not fallen in.

36.1 *cloaked*] Parrott.

---

18. *wreak*] revenge.   38. *outraging*] furious, wild (*OED*).

THARSALIO.

True, sister, but we must ride colts before we can break them,
you know.   45

LYSANDER.

This is your blind goddess Confidence.

THARSALIO.

Alas, brother, our house is decay'd, and my honest ambition
to restore it, I hope, be pardonable. My comfort is, the poet
that pens the story will write o'er my head *Magnis tamen
excidit ausis*,   50
Which, in our native idiom, lets you know,
His mind was high, though Fortune was his foe.

LYSANDER.

A good resolve, brother, to outjest disgrace. Come, I had
been on my journey but for some private speech with you.
Let's in.   55

THARSALIO.

Good brother, stay a little; help out this ragged colt out of
the ditch.

[*Uncloaks and reveals a splendid suit.*]

LYSANDER.

How now?

THARSALIO.

Now I confess my oversight; this have I purchas'd by my
confidence.   60

LYSANDER.

I like you, brother; 'tis the true garb, you know;
What wants in real worth, supply in show.

THARSALIO.

In show? Alas, 'twas even the thing itself.
I op'd my counting house and took away
These simple fragments of my treasury.   65
"Husband," my Countess cried, "take more, more yet";
Yet I, in haste to pay in part my debt

51–52.] *Reed; prose in Q*.   57.1 *Uncloaks . . . suit*] *Parrott.*

49–50. *Magnis . . . ausis*] "Though he greatly failed, more greatly dared";
part of the epitaph of Phaeton (Ovid *Metamorphoses* ii.328).

52. *Fortune . . . foe*] "Fortune My Foe" was the title of a popular song
of the day.

And prove myself a husband of her store,
Kiss'd and came off, and this time took no more—
CYNTHIA.

But, good brother—   70
THARSALIO.

—Then were our honor'd spousal rites perform'd;
We made all short, and sweet, and close, and sure—
LYSANDER.

He's rapt.
THARSALIO.

—Then did my ushers and chief servants stoop;
Then made my women curtsies, and envied   75
Their lady's fortune. I was magnified.
LYSANDER.

Let him alone; this spirit will soon vanish.
THARSALIO.

Brother and sister, as I love you and am true servant to
Venus, all the premises are serious and true, and the conclusion is, the great Countess is mine, the palace is at your   80
service, to which I invite you all to solemnize my honor'd
nuptials.
LYSANDER.

Can this be credited!
THARSALIO.

Good brother, do not you envy my fortunate achievement?
LYSANDER.

Nay, I ever said the attempt was commendable—   85
THARSALIO.

Good.
LYSANDER.

—If the issue were successful.
THARSALIO.

A good state-conclusion; happy events make good the
worst attempts. Here are your widow-vows, sister; thus are
ye all in your pure naturals. Certain moral disguises of   90
coyness, which the ignorant call modesty, ye borrow of art

73. rapt] *Dodsley;* wrap't *Q.*   84. achievement?] *Dodsley;*
                                          achievement. *Q.*
_____

88. *events*] results.

to cover your busk points, which a blunt and resolute
encounter, taken under a fortunate aspect, easily disarms
you of; and then, alas, what are you? Poor naked sinners,
God wot; weak paper walls thrust down with a finger. This   95
is the way on't, boil their appetites to a full height of lust
and then take them down in the nick.

CYNTHIA.

Is there probability in this, that a lady so great, so virtuous,
standing on so high terms of honor, should so soon stoop?

THARSALIO.

You would not wonder, sister, if you knew the lure she   100
stoop'd at. Greatness? Think you that can curb affection?
No, it whets it more. They have the full stream of blood to
bear them, the sweet gale of their sublim'd spirits to drive
them, the calm of ease to prepare them, the sunshine of
fortune to allure them, greatness to waft them safe through   105
all rocks of infamy. When youth, wit, and person come
aboard once, tell me, sister, can you choose but hoist sail
and put forward to the main?

LYSANDER.

But let me wonder at this frailty yet.
Would she in so short time wear out his memory,   110
So soon wipe from her eyes, nay, from her heart,
Whom I myself, and this whole isle besides,
Still remember with grief, the impression of his loss
Taking worthily such root in us;
How think you, wife?   115

CYNTHIA.

I am asham'd on't, and abhor to think
So great and vow'd a pattern of our sex
Should take into her thoughts, nay, to her bed
(O stain to womanhood), a second love.

LYCUS.

In so short time!

CYNTHIA.   In any time!

LYSANDER.   No, wife?   120

109–115.] *Parrott; prose in* Q.   120. No, wife?] *Reed;* No wife. Q.

___

92. *busk points*] the end of the strip of whalebone that stiffens the front
of the corset, used here metaphorically for "bosom."

CYNTHIA.

By Juno no; sooner a loathsome toad.

THARSALIO.

High words, believe me, and I think she'll keep them.
Next turn is yours, nephew; you shall now marry my noblest
lady-daughter; the first marriage in Paphos next my nuptials
shall be yours. These are strange occurrents, brother, but 125
pretty and pathetical. If you see me in my chair of honor
and my Countess in mine arms, you will then believe, I hope,
I am lord of the palace; then shall you try my great lady's
entertainment, see your hands freed of me, and mine taking
you to advancement.   130

LYSANDER.

Well, all this rids not my business. Wife, you shall be there
to partake the unexpected honor of our house. Lycus and I
will make it our recreation by the way to think of your revels
and nuptial sports. Brother, my stay hath been for you. Wife,
pray thee be gone, and soon prepare for the solemnity; a 135
month returns me.

CYNTHIA.

Heavens guide your journey.

LYSANDER.

Farewell.

THARSALIO.

Farewell, nephew; prosper in virility, but—do you hear?—
keep your hand from your voice. I have a part for you in our 140
hymeneal show.

HYLUS.

You speak too late for my voice, but I'll discharge the part.
                                        [*Exeunt*] Cynthia, Hylus, [*Ero*].

LYSANDER.

Occurrents call ye them? Foul shame confound them all!
That impregnable fort of chastity and loyalty, that amaze-
ment of the world! O ye deities, could nothing restrain her? 145
I took her spirit to be too haughty for such a depression.

142.1. *Exeunt*] *Collier; Exit Q*.   142.1. *Ero*] *Parrott*.

---

125. *occurrents*] occurrences, incidents.

THARSALIO.

But who commonly more short-heel'd than they that are
high i'th' instep?

LYSANDER.

Methinks yet shame should have controll'd so sudden an
appetite.   150

THARSALIO.

Tush, shame doth extinguish lust as oil doth fire;
The blood once het, shame doth enflame the more;
What they before by art dissembled most,
They act more freely; shame once found is lost.
And to say truth, brother, what shame is due to't? Or what 155
congruence doth it carry that a young lady, gallant, vigorous,
full of spirit and complexion, her appetite new-whetted with
nuptial delights, to be confin'd to the speculation of a
death's head; or for the loss of a husband, the world afford-
ing flesh enough, make the noontide of her years, the sunset 160
of her pleasures?

LYCUS.

And yet there have been such women.

THARSALIO.

Of the first stamp, perhaps, when the metal was purer than
in these degenerate days; of later years, much of that coin
hath been counterfeit and, besides, so crack'd and worn 165
with use that they are grown light and indeed fit for nothing
but to be turn'd over in play.

LYSANDER.

Not all, brother.

THARSALIO.

My matchless sister only excepted; for she, you know, is
made of another metal than that she borrow'd of her 170
mother. But do you, brother, sadly intend the pursuit of this
trial?

147–148. *short-heel'd . . . instep*] *Short-heel'd* often means "light," or "loose"
and signifies woman's frailty. *High in the instep* is a phrase often used to
denote pride.

151. *extinguish . . . fire*] proverbial (Tilley, F 287 and O 30).

152. *het*] old form of heated (*OED*).

171. *sadly*] seriously.

LYSANDER.

Irrevocably.

THARSALIO.

It's a high project. If it be once rais'd, the earth is too weak
to bear so weighty an accident; it cannot be conjur'd down 175
again without an earthquake. Therefore, believe she will be
constant.

LYSANDER.

No, I will not.

THARSALIO.

Then believe she will not be constant.

LYSANDER.

Neither. I will believe nothing but what trial enforces. Will 180
you hold your promise for the governing of this project with
skill and secrecy?

THARSALIO.

If it must needs be so. But hark you, brother, have you no
other capricions in your head to entrap my sister in her
frailty but to prove the firmness of her widow-vows after 185
your suppos'd death?

LYSANDER.

None in the world.

THARSALIO.

Then here's my hand; I'll be as close as my lady's shoe to
her foot, that pinches and pleases her, and will bear on with
the plot till the vessel split again.   190

LYSANDER.

Forge any death, so you can force belief.
Say I was poison'd, drown'd.

THARSALIO.   Hang'd!

LYSANDER.   Anything,

So you assist it with likely circumstance; I need not instruct
you. That must be your employment, Lycus.

LYCUS.

Well, sir.   195

THARSALIO.

But, brother, you must set in, too; to countenance truth out,
a hearse there must be too. It's strange to think how much

191–192.] *Parrott; prose in Q.*

the eye prevails in such impressions; I have mark'd a widow
that just before was seen pleasant enough, follow an empty
hearse and weep devoutly.   200

LYCUS.

All those things leave to me.

LYSANDER.

But, brother, for the bestowing of this hearse in the monument of our family, and the marshaling of a funeral—

THARSALIO.

Leave that to my care, and if I do not do the mourner as
lively as your heir, and weep as lustily as your widow, say   205
there's no virtue in onions. That being done, I'll come to
visit the distress'd widow, apply old ends of comfort to her
grief; but the burden of my song shall be to tell her words are
but dead comforts, and therefore counsel her to take a living
comfort, that might ferret out the thought of her dead hus-   210
band; and will come prepar'd with choice of suitors, either
my Spartan lord for grace at the Viceroy's Court, or some
great lawyer that may solder up her crack'd estate, and so
forth. But what would you say, brother, if you should find
her married at your arrival?   215

LYSANDER.

By this hand, split her weasand.

THARSALIO.

Well, forget not your wager, a stately chariot with four
brave horses of the Thracian breed, with all appurtenances.
I'll prepare the like for you, if you prove victor. But well
remember'd, where will you lurk the whiles?   220

LYSANDER.

Mew'd up close, some short day's journey hence;
Lycus shall know the place; write still how all things pass.
Brother, adieu; all joy attend you.

THARSALIO.

Will you not stay, our nuptial now so near?

LYSANDER.

I should be like a man that hears a tale   225

---

216. *weasand*] throat.
218. *Thracian breed*] Thracian horses were esteemed.
221. *Mew'd*] confined, a term from falconry.

And heeds it not, one absent from himself.
My wife shall attend the Countess, and my son.

THARSALIO.

Whom you shall hear at your return call me
Father. Adieu; Jove be your speed.
My nuptials done, your funerals succeed.   *Exeunt.* 230

[III.ii]   *Enter* Argus, *barehead.*

ARGUS.

A hall, a hall! Who's without there?   (*Enter two or three with
cushions.*)   Come on, y'are proper grooms, are ye not?
'Slight, I think y'are all bridegrooms, ye take your pleasures
so. A company of dormice. Their honors are upon coming,
and the room not ready. Rushes and seats instantly!   5

                    [*Enter* Tharsalio.]

THARSALIO.

Now alas, fellow Argus, how thou art cumber'd with an
office!

ARGUS.

Perfume, sirrah, the room's dampish.

THARSALIO.

Nay, you may leave that office to the ladies; they'll perfume
it sufficiently.   10

ARGUS [*perceiving* Tharsalio].

Cry mercy, sir, here's a whole chorus of Sylvans at hand,
cornetting, and tripping o'th' toe, as the ground they trod
on were too hot for their feet. The device is rare. And there's
your young nephew, too; he hangs in the clouds deified with
Hymen's shape.   15

THARSALIO.

Is he perfect in's part? Has not his tongue learn'd of the
Sylvans to trip o' th' toe?

228. hear] *Dodsley;* here *Q.*   5.1 *Enter* Tharsalio] *Parrott.*
226–229.] *Parrott; prose in Q.*   11. S.D. *perceiving* Tharsalio]
[III.ii]   *Parrott.*

1. *A hall, a hall!*] a cry frequently employed to make room for a
mask.
5. *Rushes*] It was customary to strew the floor with rushes.

ARGUS.

> Sir, believe it, he does it preciously for accent and action, as
> if he felt the part he play'd. He ravishes all the young
> wenches in the palace; pray Venus my young lady Laodice   20
> have not some little prick of Cupid in her, she's so diligent
> at's rehearsals.

THARSALIO.

> No force, so my next vows be heard, that if Cupid have
> prick'd her, Hymen may cure her.

ARGUS.

> You mean your nephew, sir, that presents Hymen.   25

THARSALIO.

> Why so. I can speak nothing but thou art within me. Fie of
> this wit of thine, 'twill be thy destruction. But howsoever you
> please to understand, Hymen send the boy no worse fortune.
> And where's my lady's honor?

ARGUS.

> At hand, sir, with your unparagon'd sister. Please you take   30
> your chair of honor, sir?

THARSALIO.

> Most serviceable Argus, the gods reward thy service, for I
> will not.

Enter Eudora, *leading* Cynthia; Laodice, Sthenia, *Ianthe, Ero, with
others following.*

EUDORA.

> Come, sister, now we must exchange that name
> For stranger titles, let's dispose ourselves   35
> To entertain these Sylvan revelers,
> That come to grace our loved nuptials.
> I fear me we must all turn nymphs tonight,
> To side those sprightly wood-gods in their dances;
> Can you do't nimbly, sister? 'Slight, what ails you,   40
> Are you not well?

24. may] *Dodsley;* my *Q*.   40–43.] *Reed; prose in Q*.
40. ails] *Parrott;* aile *Q*.

---

26. *within me*] "inside my guard," a phrase from fencing (Parrott).
34–35. *exchange . . . titles*] mutually use the name of sister in place of
more distant terms of address.
39. *To side*] to walk beside.

CYNTHIA.   Yes, madam.

EUDORA.   But your looks,
Methinks, are cloudy, suiting ill the sunshine
Of this clear honor to your husband's house.
Is there ought here that sorts not with your liking?

THARSALIO.

Blame her not, mistress, if her looks show care.   45
Excuse the merchant's sadness that hath made
A doubtful venture of his whole estate,
His livelihood, his hopes, in one poor bottom,
To all encounters of the sea and storms.
Had you a husband that you lov'd as well,   50
Would you not take his absent plight as ill?
Cavil at every fancy? Not an object
That could present itself, but it would forge
Some vain objection that did doubt his safety;
True love is ever full of jealousy.   55

EUDORA.

Jealous! Of what? Of every little journey?
Mere fancy then is wanton, and doth cast
At those slight dangers there too doting glances;
Misgiving minds ever provoke mischances.
Shines not the sun in his way bright as here?   60
Is not the air as good? What hazard doubt you?

ARGUS.

His horse may stumble, if it please your honor;
The rain may wet, the wind may blow on him;
Many shrewd hazards watch poor travelers.

EUDORA.

True, and the shrewdest thou hast reckon'd us.   65
Good sister, these cares fit young married wives.

CYNTHIA.

Wives should be still young in their husband's loves.
Time bears no scythe should bear down them before him;

42. suiting ill] *Shepherd;* suiting all
Q.

46–48. *merchant's . . . bottom*] an adaptation of the proverb "Venture
not all in one bottom" (Tilley, A 209).
55. *True . . . jealousy*] proverbial (Tilley, L 510).

Our lives he may cut short, but not our loves.

THARSALIO.

    Sister, be wise, and ship not in one bark   70
    All your ability. If he miscarry,
    Your well-tried wisdom should look out for new.

CYNTHIA.

    I wish them happy winds that run that course;
    From me 'tis far. One temple seal'd our troth;
    One tomb, one hour shall end, and shroud us both.   75

THARSALIO.

    Well, y'are a Phoenix; there, be that your cheer;
    Love with your husband be, your wisdom here.
    Hark, our sports challenge it. Sit, dearest mistress.

EUDORA.

    Take your place, worthiest servant.

THARSALIO.   Serve me heaven,   *Music.*
    As I my heavenly mistress. Sit, rare sister.   80

Music. [Hylus *as*] Hymen *descends, and six Sylvans enter beneath, with torches.*

ARGUS.

    A hall, a hall! Let no more citizens in there.

LAODICE.

    O, not my cousin see, but Hymen's self.

STHENIA.

    He does become it most enflamingly.

HYMEN.

    Hail, honor'd bridegroom, and his princely bride,
    With the most fam'd for virtue, Cynthia;   85

---

72. out] *Dodsley;* ont *Q.*   80.1. Hylus *as*] *this edn.*

80.1.] Hymen (Hylus) presumably descends by means of a piece of stage machinery (cf. Chambers, *Elizabethan Stage*, III, 132, n. 3). Irwin Smith (*Shakespeare's Blackfriars Playhouse*, New York, 1964, pp. 415–416) suggests that he descended from the third or uppermost level of the Blackfriars stage, where, to judge from III.ii.13–15 ("And there's your young nephew, too; he hangs in the clouds deified with Hymen's shape."), the boy is visible aloft for some time before his descent begins. "He does not alight upon the stage; instead, his descent is halted at such a level that '*six Sylvans enter beneath, with torches*'" (Smith, p. 416).

And this young lady, bright Laodice,
One rich hope of this noblest family.

STHENIA.

Hark how he courts; he is enamor'd, too.

LAODICE.

O grant it, Venus, and be ever honor'd.

HYMEN.

In grace and love of you, I Hymen search'd   90
The groves and thickets that embrace this palace,
With this clear-flam'd and good-aboding torch,
For summons of these fresh and flowery Sylvans
To this fair presence, with their winding hays,
Active and antic dances, to delight   95
Your frolic eyes and help to celebrate
These noblest nuptials, which great Destiny
Ordain'd past custom and all vulgar object
To be the readvancement of a house,
Noble and princely, and restore this palace   100
To that name that six hundred summers since
Was in possession of this bridegroom's ancestors,
The ancient and most virtue-fam'd Lysandri.
Sylvans! The courtships you make to your Dryads,
Use to this great bride and these other dames,   105
And heighten with your sports my nuptial flames.

LAODICE.

O, would himself descend, and me command.

STHENIA.

Dance, and his heart catch in another's hand.

Sylvans take out the Bride and the rest; they dance; after which, and all set in their places, Hymen [*speaks*].

HYMEN.

Now, what the power and my torch's influence
Hath in the blessings of your nuptial joys,   110
Great bride and bridegroom, you shall amply part

108.2. *speaks*] *Parrott.*

---

94. *hays*] country dances, of the nature of reels.
98. *past custom*] "above conventions" (Parrott).
98. *vulgar object*] "popular, ordinary, objections" (Parrott).

Betwixt your free loves, and forego it never.

OMNES.

Thanks to great Hymen and fair Sylvans ever.   *Exeunt.*

Finis Actus Tertii.

[IV.i]

[*Enter*] Tharsalio, Lycus, *with his arm in a scarf, a nightcap on's head.*

LYCUS.

I hope, sir, by this time—

THARSALIO.

Put on, man, by ourselves.

LYCUS.

—The edge of your confidence is well taken off. Would
you not be content to withdraw your wager?

THARSALIO.

Faith, fellow Lycus, if my wager were weakly built, this   5
unexpected accident might stagger it. For the truth is, this
strain is extraordinary, to follow her husband's body into
the tomb, and there for his company to bury herself quick.
It's new and stirring; but for all this, I'll not despair of my
wager.   10

LYCUS.

Why, sir, can you think such a passion dissembl'd?

THARSALIO.

All's one for that; what I think, I think. In the meantime,
forget not to write to my brother how the plot hath succeeded: that the news of his death hath taken; a funeral
solemnity perform'd; his suppos'd corse bestow'd in the   15
monument of our family; thou and I horrible mourners; but
above all, that his intolerable virtuous widow, for his love,
and (for her love) Ero, her handmaid, are descended with
his corse into the vault; there wipe their eyes time out of
mind, drink nothing but their own tears, and by this time are 20
almost dead with famine. There's a point will sting it (for you
say 'tis true). Where left you him?

[IV.i]

A week has passed since Act III. According to l. 112, below, Cynthia has
been in the tomb for four days (Parrott).

2. *Put on*] put on your cap.

LYCUS.

    At Dipolis, sir, some twenty miles hence.

THARSALIO.

    He keeps close.

LYCUS.

    Ay, sir, by all means; skulks unknown under the name of a   25
strange knight.

THARSALIO.

    That may carry him without descrying, for there's a number
of strange knights abroad. You left him well?

LYCUS.

    Well, sir, but for this jealous humor that haunts him.

THARSALIO.

    Well, this news will absolutely purge that humor. Write all;   30
forget not to describe her passion at thy discovery of his
slaughter. Did she perform it well for her husband's wager?

LYCUS.

    Perform it, call you it? You may jest; men hunt hares to
death for their sports, but the poor beasts die in earnest.
You wager of her passions for your pleasure, but she takes   35
little pleasure in those earnest passions. I never saw such an
ecstasy of sorrow since I knew the name of sorrow. Her hands
flew up to her head like Furies, hid all her beauties in her
dishevel'd hair, and wept as she would turn fountain. I
would you and her husband had been behind the arras but   40
to have heard her. I assure you, sir, I was so transported
with the spectacle that, in despite of my discretion, I was
forc'd to turn woman and bear a part with her. Humanity
broke loose from my heart, and stream'd through mine
eyes.   45

THARSALIO.

    In prose, thou wept'st. So have I seen many a moist
auditor do at a play when the story was but a mere fiction.
And didst act the Nuntius well? Would I had heard it!
Could'st thou dress thy looks in a mournful habit?

---

    23. *Dipolis*] There is no such town in Cyprus. "There is a Syrian town
of this name mentioned by Pliny, *Nat. Hist.*, V, 79, and it is sometimes
applied to Lemnos" (Parrott).

    28. *strange knights*] probably a reference to the numerous new knights
created by James I.

    48. *Nuntius*] the narrator in Greek and Roman tragedy.

LYCUS.

    Not without preparation, sir, no more than my speech.   50
    'Twas a plain acting of an interlude to me to pronounce the
    part.

THARSALIO.

    As how, for heaven's sake?

LYCUS.

    "Phoebus address'd his chariot towards the west
    To change his wearied coursers," and so forth.   55

THARSALIO.

    Nay on, and thou lov'st me.

LYCUS.

    "Lysander and myself beguil'd the way
    With interchang'd discourse, but our chief theme
    Was of your dearest self, his honor'd wife,
    Your love, your virtue, wondrous constancy."   60

THARSALIO.

    Then was her cue to whimper; on.

LYCUS.

    "When suddenly appear'd as far as sight,
    A troop of horse, arm'd, as we might discern,
    With javelins, spears, and such accouterments.
    He doubted nought (as innocency ever   65
    Is free from doubting ill)."

THARSALIO.   There dropp'd a tear.

LYCUS.

    "My mind misgave me;
    They might be mountaineers. At their approach
    They us'd no other language but their weapons
    To tell us what they were. Lysander drew   70
    And bore himself Achilles-like in fight;
    And as a mower sweeps off th' heads of bents,
    So did Lysander's sword shave off the points
    Of their assaulting lances.
    His horse at last, sore hurt, fell under him;   75
    I, seeing I could not rescue, us'd my spurs
    To fly away."

77–78.] *Parrott; prose in Q.*

65–66. *He . . . ill*] proverbial (Tilley, T 221).
72. *bents*] "various grass-like reeds, rushes, sedges, etc." (*OED*).

THARSALIO.   What, from thy friend?

LYCUS.

Ay, in a good quarrel, why not?

THARSALIO.   Good, I am answer'd.

LYCUS.

"A lance pursued me, brought me back again,
And with these wounds left me t'accompany   80
Dying Lysander. Then they rifl'd us
And left us.
They gone, my breath not yet gone, 'gan to strive
And revive sense. I with my feeble joints
Crawl'd to Lysander, stirr'd him, and withal   85
He gasp'd, cried 'Cynthia!' and breath'd no more."

THARSALIO.

O, then she howl'd outright.

LYCUS.

"Passengers came and in a chariot brought us
Straight to a neighbor town, where I forthwith
Coffin'd my friend in lead, and so convey'd him   90
To this sad place."

THARSALIO.

'Twas well, and could not show but strangely.

LYCUS.

Well, sir, this tale pronounc'd with terror, suited with
action, clothed with such likely circumstance, my wounds
in show, her husband's hearse in sight, think what effect it   95
wrought. And if you doubt, let the sad consequence of her
retreat to his tomb be your woeful instructor.

THARSALIO.

For all this, I'll not despair of my wager.
These griefs that sound so loud, prove always light;
True sorrow evermore keeps out of sight.   100
This strain of mourning wi' th' sepulcher, like an overdoing
actor, affects grossly, and is indeed so far forc'd from the life,
that it bewrays itself to be altogether artificial. To set open

98–99.] *Dodsley;* For . . . These/   101. wi' th'] *conj. Brereton, accepted*
Grieues . . . light, *Q.*   *Parrott;* with *Q.*

---

103. *bewrays*] reveals, exposes.

a shop of mourning! 'Tis palpable. Truth, the substance,
hunts not after the shadow of popular fame. Her officious 105
ostentation of sorrow condemns her sincerity. When did
ever woman mourn so unmeasurably, but she did dissemble?

LYCUS.

O gods! A passion thus borne, thus apparell'd with tears,
sighs, swoonings, and all the badges of true sorrow, to be
dissembl'd! By Venus, I am sorry I ever set foot in't. Could 110
she, if she dissembl'd, thus dally with hunger, be deaf to the
barking of her appetite, not having these four days reliev'd
nature with one dram of sustenance?

THARSALIO.

For this does she look to be deified, to have hymns made of
her, nay to her; the tomb where she is, to be no more reputed 115
the ancient monument of our family, the Lysandri, but the
new-erected altar of Cynthia, to which all the Paphian
widows shall after their husbands' funerals offer their wet
muckinders for monuments of the danger they have pass'd,
as seamen do their wet garments at Neptune's temple after 120
a shipwrack.

LYCUS.

Well, I'll apprehend you at your pleasure. I for my part
will say that if her faith be as constant as her love is hearty
and unaffected, her virtues may justly challenge a deity to
enshrine them.   125

THARSALIO.

Ay, there's another point, too. But one of those virtues is
enough at once. All natures are not capable of all gifts.
If the brain of the West were in the heads of the learned,
then might parish clerks be common councilmen, and poets
aldermen's deputies. My sister may turn Niobe for love; but 130
till Niobe be turn'd to a marble, I'll not despair but she
may prove a woman. Let the trial run on; if she do not out-
run it, I'll say poets are no prophets, prognosticators are but
mountebanks, and none tell true but woodmongers.   *Exit.*

LYCUS.

A sweet gentleman you are! I marvel what man, what 135

---

119. *muckinders*] handerkerchiefs.

woman, what name, what action, doth his tongue glide over,
but it leaves a slime upon't! Well, I'll presently to Dipolis,
where Lysander stays, and will not say but she may prove
frail.

But this I'll say, if she should chance to break,   140
Her tears are true, though women's truths are weak.   *Exit.*

[IV.ii]

Enter Lysander *like a Soldier, disguis'd at all parts, a half pike, gorget, etc.*
He discovers the tomb, looks in, and wonders, etc.

LYSANDER.

   O miracle of Nature! Women's glory,
   Men's shame, and envy of the deities!
   Yet must these matchless creatures be suspected,
   Accus'd, condemn'd! Now by th'immortal gods,
   They rather merit altars, sacrifice,   5
   Than love and courtship.
   Yet see, the queen of these lies here interred,
   Tearing her hair and drowned in her tears,
   Which Jove should turn to crystal, and a mirror
   Make of them, wherein men may see and wonder   10
   At women's virtues. Shall she famish then?
   Will men (without dissuasions) suffer thus
   So bright an ornament to earth, tomb'd quick
   In earth's dark bosom? Ho! Who's in the tomb there?

ERO [*within*].

   Who calls? Whence are you?   15

LYSANDER.

   I am a soldier of the watch and must enter.

140–141.] *Dodsley; prose in Q.*   as separate line.
[IV.ii]   14. Who's . . . there?] *Collier;* Q
1. S.P. LYSANDER] *Dodsley; not in Q.*   prints as separate line.
4. Now . . . gods] *Collier; Q prints*   15. S.D. within] *Parrott.*

[IV.ii]
   From this scene until the end of the play, all the action takes place
either in the Lysandri tomb, or in the graveyard around it. I visualize the
inner stage representing the tomb, where the action involving Cynthia
takes place, except for IV.iii, when she and Ero step outside for a few
minutes before Lysander returns.

ERO.

    Amongst the dead?

LYSANDER.

    Do the dead speak? Ope, or I'll force it open.

ERO [*opening the door of the tomb*].

    What violence is this? What seek you here,

    Where nought but Death and her attendants dwell?   20

LYSANDER.

    What wretched souls are you that thus by night

    Lurk here amongst the dead?

ERO.   Good soldier, do not stir her.

    She's weak and quickly seiz'd with swooning and passions,

    And with much trouble shall we both recall

    Her fainting spirits.   25

    Five days thus hath she wasted, and not once

    Season'd her palate with the taste of meat;

    Her powers of life are spent, and what remains

    Of her famish'd spirit serves not to breathe but sigh.

    She hath exil'd her eyes from sleep or sight,   30

    And given them wholly up to ceaseless tears

    Over that ruthful hearse of her dear spouse,

    Slain by bandittoes, nobly born Lysander.

LYSANDER.

    And hopes she with these heavy notes and cries

    To call him from the dead? In these five days   35

    Hath she but made him stir a finger or fetch

    One gasp of that forsaken life she mourns?

    Come, honor'd mistress, I admire your virtues,

    But must reprove this vain excess of moan.

    Rouse yourself, lady, and look up from death.   40

    Well said, 'tis well; stay by my hand and rise.

    This face hath been maintain'd with better huswifery.

CYNTHIA [*at the door of the tomb*].

    What are you?

---

19. S.D. *opening . . . tomb*] *Parrott.*   29. breathe] *Dodsley;* breath *Q*.
21–22.] *Reed; prose in Q*.   30–37.] *Collier; prose in Q*.
22–29.] *Parrott; prose in Q*.   43. S.D. *at . . . tomb*] *Parrott.*

---

    42. *huswifery*] "house-keeping, with special reference to the table" (Parrott).

LYSANDER.   Lady, I am sentinel,
Set in this hallowed place to watch and guard,
On forfeit of my life, these monuments   45
From rape and spoil of sacrilegious hands;
And save the bodies, that without you see,
Of crucified offenders, that no friends
May bear them hence to honor'd burial.

CYNTHIA.
Thou seem'st an honest soldier; pray thee then,   50
Be as thou seem'st; betake thee to thy charge
And leave this place; add not affliction
To the afflicted.

LYSANDER.   You misname the children.
For what you term affliction now, in you
Is but self-humor, voluntary penance   55
Impos'd upon yourself; and you lament
As did the Satyr once, that ran affrighted
From that horn's sound that he himself had winded;
Which humor to abate, my counsel tending your term'd
     affliction,
What I for physic give, you take for poison.   60
I tell you, honor'd mistress, these ingredients
Are wholesome, though perhaps they seem untoothsome.

ERO [aside].
This soldier, sure, is some decay'd pothecary.

LYSANDER.
Dear ghost, be wise and pity your fair self,
Thus by yourself unnaturally afflicted.   65
Chide back heartbreaking groans, clear up those lamps,
Restore them to their first creation,
Windows for light, not sluices made for tears.
Beat not the senseless air with needless cries,
Baneful to life and bootless to the dead.   70

46. spoil] *Dodsley;* spoil'd *Q.*

---

51. *Be . . . seem'st*] proverb, "Be what thou would seem to be" (Tilley, S 214).

57–58. *Satyr . . . winded*] In the 1598 edition of the *Arcadia* is a sonnet by Dyer "on the theme of a satyr who kissed the fire he saw for the first time. This is followed by a sonnet of Sidney's beginning: '*A satyr once did run away for dread/ With sound of horn which he himself did blow*'" (Parrott).

This is the inn where all Deucalion's race
Sooner or later must take up their lodging;
No privilege can free us from this prison;
No tears, no prayers, can redeem from hence
A captiv'd soul. Make use of what you see;   75
Let this affrighting spectacle of death
Teach you to nourish life.

ERO.

Good, hear him. This is a rare soldier.

LYSANDER.

Say that with abstinence you should unloose
The knot of life. Suppose that in this tomb   80
For your dear spouse you should entomb yourself
A living corse; say that before your hour,
Without due summons from the Fates, you send
Your hasty soul to hell; can your dear spouse
Take notice of your faith and constancy?   85
Shall your dear spouse revive to give you thanks?

CYNTHIA.

Idle discourser.

LYSANDER.   No, your moans are idle.
Go to, I say, be counsel'd. Raise yourself;
Enjoy the fruits of life; there's viands for you.
Now, live for a better husband. No? Will you none?   90

ERO.

For love of courtesy, good mistress, eat;
Do not reject so kind and sweet an offer.
Who knows but this may be some Mercury
Disguis'd, and sent from Juno to relieve us?
Did ever any lend unwilling ears   95
To those that came with messages of life?

CYNTHIA.

I pray thee, leave thy rhetoric.

79–86.] *Reed; prose in Q.*   90. No . . . none?] *Parrott; Q prints
                                        as separate line.*

---

71. *Deucalion's race*] Deucalion was the Greek Noah. He and his wife
Pyrrha were the only survivors after Zeus inundated the world. The two
repeopled the earth by throwing stones over their shoulders; from the
stones sprang up men and women.
    82. *corse*] corpse.

ERO.

> By my soul, to speak plain truth, I could rather wish t'employ
> my teeth than my tongue, so your example would be my
> warrant.   100

CYNTHIA.

> Thou hast my warrant.

LYSANDER.   Well then, eat, my wench;

> Let obstinacy starve. Fall to.

ERO.   Persuade

> My mistress first.

LYSANDER.   'Slight, tell me, lady,

> Are you resolv'd to die? If that be so,
> Choose not (for shame) a base and beggar's death;   105
> Die not for hunger, like a Spartan lady;
> Fall valiantly upon a sword, or drink
> Noble death; expel your grief with poison.
> There 'tis, seize it. [*Offering his sword.*]   Tush, you dare
>   not die.
> Come, wench, thou hast not lost a husband;   110
> Thou shalt eat. Th'art now within
> The place where I command.

ERO.   I protest, sir—

LYSANDER.

> Well said. Eat and protest; or I'll protest,
> And do thou eat. Thou eat'st against thy will,
> That's it thou would'st say?   115

ERO.

> It is.

LYSANDER.   And under such a protestation

> Thou lost thy maidenhead.
> For your own sake, good lady, forget this husband.
> Come, you are now become a happy widow,
> A blessedness that many would be glad of.   120
> That and your husband's inventory together
> Will raise you up husbands enow. What think you of me?

CYNTHIA.

> Trifler, pursue this wanton theme no further,

Lest (which I would be loath) your speech provoke
Uncivil language from me. I must tell you,   125
One joint of him I lost was much more worth
Than the rack'd value of thy entire body.

ERO.

O know what joint she means.

LYSANDER.   Well, I have done.
And well done, frailty. Proface! How lik'st thou it?

ERO.

Very toothsome ingredients surely, sir;   130
Want but some liquor to incorporate them.

LYSANDER.

There 'tis; carouse.

ERO.   I humbly thank you, sir.

LYSANDER.

Hold, pledge me now!

ERO.   'Tis the poison, sir,
That preserves life, I take it.   *Bibit Ancilla.*

LYSANDER.   Do so, take it.

ERO.

Sighing has made me something short-winded.   135
I'll pledge y'at twice.

LYSANDER.   'Tis well done; do me right.

ERO.

I pray, sir, have you been a pothecary?

LYSANDER.

Marry have I, wench; a woman's pothecary.

ERO.

Have you good ingredients?
I like your bottle well. Good mistress, taste it.   140
Try but the operation, 'twill fetch up
The roses in your cheeks again.
Doctor Verolles' bottles are not like it;

---

127. *rack'd value*] "the value strained, or raised above the normal" (Parrott).

129. *Proface*] much good may it do you, or may it do you good, a formula of welcome or good wishes at a meal, or a toast drunk to one's health (*OED*).

134. S.D. *Bibit Ancilla*] The maid drinks.

136. *do me right*] an expression used in pledging healths.

There's no guaiacum here, I can assure you.

LYSANDER.

This will do well anon.

ERO.   Now fie upon't.   145

O, I have lost my tongue in this same limbo.
The spring on't's spoil'd, methinks; it goes not off
With the old twang.

LYSANDER.

Well said, wench, oil it well; 'twill make it slide well.

ERO.

Aristotle says, sir, in his *Posterionds*—   150

LYSANDER.

This wench is learned. —And what says he?

ERO.

—That when a man dies, the last thing that moves is his
heart; in a woman, her tongue.

LYSANDER.

Right, and adds further that you women are
A kind of spinners; if their legs be pluck'd off,   155
Yet still they'll wag them; so will you your tongues.
[*Aside*.]   With what an easy change does this same weakness
Of women slip from one extreme t'another!
All these attractions take no hold of her,
No, not to take refection; 't must not be thus.—   160
Well said, wench. Tickle that Helicon.
But shall we quit the field with this disgrace
Given to our oratory? Both not gain
So much ground of her as to make her eat?

ERO.

Faith, the truth is, sir, you are no fit organ   165
For this business;

147. on't's] *Parrott;* ants *Q.*   154–156.] *Reed; prose in Q.*

144. *guaiacum*] a drug prepared from the resin of guaiacum tree (Parrott).
146. *limbo*] a place of confinement.
150. *Posterionds*] error for Aristotle's *Analytica Posteriora* (Parrott).
155. *spinners*] spiders.
160. *refection*] refreshment (*OED*).
161. *Helicon*] a mountain in Boeotia, sacred to the Muses. The fountain
Aganippe, located there, was believed to inspire anyone who drank of its
waters. Lysander jests that the liquor has inspired Ero's erudition.

'Tis quite out of your element.
Let us alone, she'll eat, I have no fear;
A woman's tongue best fits a woman's ear.
Jove never did employ Mercury,   170
But Iris, for his messenger to Juno.

LYSANDER.

Come, let me kiss thee, wench. Wilt undertake
To make thy mistress eat?

ERO.   It shall go hard, sir,
But I will make her turn flesh and blood,
And learn to live as other mortals do.   175

LYSANDER.

Well said. The morning hastes; next night expect me.

ERO.

With more provision, good sir.

LYSANDER.   Very good.   *Exiturus.*

ERO.

And bring more wine.   *She shuts up the tomb.*

LYSANDER.   What else? Shalt have enough.
O Cynthia, heir of her bright purity
Whose name thou dost inherit, thou disdain'st   180
(Sever'd from all concretion) to feed
Upon the base food of gross elements.
Thou all art soul, all immortality.
Thou fasts for nectar and ambrosia,   .
Which, till thou find'st and eat'st above the stars,   185
To all food here thou bidd'st celestial wars.   *Exit.*

[IV.iii]   Cynthia, Ero, *the tomb opening.*

ERO.

So; let's air our dampish spirits, almost stifl'd in this gross,
muddy element.

CYNTHIA.

How sweet a breath the calmness of the night
Inspires the air withal!

3–4.] *Collier; prose in* Q.

---

181. *concretion*] a solid mass of material substance.
[IV.iii]
This scene takes place twenty-four hours later (Parrott).

ERO.

> Well said, now y'are yourself. Did not I tell you how sweet   5
> an operation the soldier's bottle had? And if there be such
> virtue in the bottle, what is there in the soldier? Know and
> acknowledge his worth when he comes, in any case, mistress.

CYNTHIA.

> So, maid?

ERO.

> God's my patience! Did you look, forsooth, that Juno should   10
> have sent you meat from her own trencher in reward of your
> widow's tears? You might sit and sigh first till your heart-
> strings broke, I'll able't.

CYNTHIA.

> I fear me thy lips have gone so oft to the bottle, that thy
> tongue-strings are come broken home.   15

ERO.

> Faith, the truth is my tongue hath been so long tied up that
> 'tis cover'd with rust, and I rub it against my palate as we
> do suspected coins, to try whether it be current or no. But
> now, mistress, for an upshot of this bottle; let's have one
> carouse to the good speed of my old master, and the good   20
> speed of my new.

CYNTHIA.

> So, damsel.

ERO.

> You must pledge it; here's to it. Do me right, I pray.

CYNTHIA.

> You say I must.   [*She drinks.*]

ERO.

> Must! What else!   25

CYNTHIA.

> How excellent ill this humor suits our habit!

ERO.

> Go to, mistress, do not think but you and I shall have good
> sport with this jest when we are in private at home. I would
> to Venus we had some honest shift or other to get off withal,

24. S.D. *She drinks*] Parrott.

---

13. *able't*] See II.iii.2, note.
19. *for an upshot*] to finish off (Parrott).

for I'll no more on't; I'll not turn saltpeter in this vault for 30
never a man's company living, much less for a woman's. Sure
I am the wonder's over, and 'twas only for that, that I
endur'd this; and so, o' my conscience, did you. Never deny
it.

CYNTHIA.

Nay, pray thee take it to thee.   35

Enter Lysander.

Hark, I hear some footing near us.

ERO.

God's me, 'tis the soldier, mistress. By Venus, if you fall to
your late black Sanctus again, I'll discover you.

LYSANDER [*aside*].

What's here! The maid hath certainly prevail'd with her;
methinks those clouds that last night cover'd her looks are 40
now dispers'd. I'll try this further. —Save you, lady.

ERO.

Honorable soldier! Y'are welcome; please you step in, sir?

LYSANDER.

With all my heart, sweetheart; by your patience, lady. Why
this bears some shape of life yet! Damsel, th'ast perform'd a
service of high reckoning, which cannot perish unrewarded. 45

ERO.

Faith, sir, you are in the way to do it once, if you have the
heart to hold on.

CYNTHIA.

Your bottle has poison'd this wench, sir.

LYSANDER.

A wholesome poison it is, lady, if I may be judge; of which
sort here is one better bottle more.   50
    Wine is ordain'd to raise such hearts as sink;
    Whom woeful stars distemper, let him drink.
I am most glad I have been some mean to this part of your

36.] *Q heads line with repetition of S.P.*   39. S.D. *aside*] *Parrott.*
"*Cyn.*"

35. *take it to thee*] i.e., speak for yourself.
38. *black Sanctus*] originally a parody of the hymn "*Sanctus, Sanctus,
Sanctus.*" "'To sing the black Sanctus' was an Elizabethan phrase equivalent
to 'lament one's case.'" (Parrott).

recovery, and will drink to the rest of it.

ERO.

Go to, mistress, pray simper no more; pledge the man of 55
war here.

CYNTHIA.

Come, y'are too rude.

ERO.

Good.

LYSANDER.

Good sooth, lady, y'are honor'd in her service; I would have
you live, and she would have you live freely, without which 60
life is but death. To live freely is to feast our appetites freely,
without which humans are stones; to the satisfaction where-
of I drink, lady.

CYNTHIA.

I'll pledge you, sir.   [*She drinks.*]

ERO.

Said like a mistress, and the mistress of yourself. Pledge 65
him in love, too; I see he loves you. She's silent, she consents,
sir.

LYSANDER.

O happy stars! And now pardon, lady. [*Kisses her.*]
Methinks these are all of a piece.

ERO.

Nay, if you kiss all of a piece, we shall ne'er have done. Well, 70
'twas well offer'd, and as well taken.

CYNTHIA.

If the world should see this!

LYSANDER.

The world! Should one so rare as yourself respect the
vulgar world?

CYNTHIA.

The praise I have had, I would continue.   75

LYSANDER.

What, of the vulgar? Who hates not the vulgar deserves not
love of the virtuous. And to affect praise of that we despise,
how ridiculous it is!

64. S.D. *She drinks*] Parrott.   68. S.D. *Kisses her*] Parrott.

---

70. *all of a piece*] all of the same kind.

ERO.

Comfortable doctrine, mistress; edify, edify! Methinks even
thus it was when Dido and Aeneas met in the cave. And hark,   80
methinks I hear some of the hunters.   *She shuts the tomb.*

Finis Actus Quarti.

[V.i]   *Enter* Tharsalio, Lycus.

LYCUS.

'Tis such an obstinacy in you, sir,
As never was conceited, to run on
With an opinion against all the world
And what your eyes may witness; to adventure
The famishment for grief of such a woman   5
As all men's merits, met in any one,
Could not deserve.

THARSALIO.   I must confess it, Lycus;
We'll therefore now prevent it if we may.
And that our curious trial hath not dwelt
Too long on this unnecessary haunt,   10
Grief and all want of food not having wrought
Too mortally on her divine disposure—

LYCUS.

I fear they have, and she is past our cure—

THARSALIO.

I must confess with fear and shame as much.

LYCUS.

—And that she will not trust in anything   15
What you persuade her to.

79–81.] *Shepherd;* Comfortable . . .   . . . hearke/ Me . . . hunters. *Q*.
edifie./ Me thinkes . . . *Dido*/ And

---

80. *Dido . . . cave*] Hardin Craig notes that in *The Tempest*, II.i.74–84,
the drunken conversation between Antonio and Sebastian concerning
the "widow Dido" is a "possible topical reference to Chapman's *Widow's
Tears*, or some other play" (*The Complete Works of Shakespeare*, 1951).
[V.i]
    "This scene is apparently continuous in time with IV.iii, for Tharsalio
on his opening the tomb (l. 22) finds Lysander in Cynthia's arms" (Parrott).
    9. *curious*] exacting.
    10. *haunt*] practice (*OED*).   12. *disposure*] disposition.

THARSALIO.   Then thou shalt haste
And call my brother from his secret shroud,
Where he appointed thee to come and tell him
How all things have succeeded.

LYCUS.   This is well
If, as I say, the ill be not so grown   20
That all help is denied her. But I fear
The matchless dame is famish'd.

                       Tharsalio *looks into the tomb.*
THARSALIO.   'Slight, who's here?
A soldier with my sister? Wipe, wipe, see,
Kissing, by Jove; she, as I lay, 'tis she.

LYCUS.
What! Is she well, sir?

THARSALIO.   O no, she is famish'd;   25
She's past our comfort; she lies drawing on.

LYCUS.
The gods forbid!

THARSALIO.   Look thou, she's drawing on.
How say'st thou?

LYCUS.   Drawing on? Illustrious witchcrafts!

THARSALIO.
Lies she not drawing on?

LYCUS.   She draws on fairly.
Your sister, sir? This she? Can this be she?   30

THARSALIO.
She, she, she, and none but she.   *He dances and sings.*
She, only queen of love and chastity;
O chastity, this women be.

LYCUS.
'Slight, 'tis prodigious.

THARSALIO.   Horse, horse, horse,
Four chariot horses of the Thracian breed   35

30. Your] *Parrott;* Our *Q.*

---

24. *lay*] wagered.
26. *drawing on*] a pun on "dying" and "enticing." For the sexual impli-
cations of the word, see Eric Partridge, *Shakespeare's Bawdy* (New York,
1960), p. 104.

Come bring me, brother. O the happiest evening
That ever drew her veil before the sun!
Who is't, canst tell?

LYCUS.   The soldier, sir, that watches
The bodies crucified in this hallow'd place
Of which to lose one, it is death to him;   40
And yet the lustful knave is at his venery,
While one might steal one.

THARSALIO.   What a slave was I
That held not out my mind's strength constantly
That she would prove thus! O incredible!
A poor eightpenny soldier! She that lately   45
Was at such height of interjection,
Stoop now to such a base conjunction!
By heaven I wonder, now I see't in act,
My brain could ever dream of such a thought.
And yet 'tis true. Rare, peerless, is't not, Lycus?   50

LYCUS.
I know not what it is, nor what to say.

THARSALIO.
O had I held out (villain that I was)
My blessed confidence but one minute longer,
I should have been eterniz'd. God's my fortune,
What an unspeakable sweet sight it is!   55
O eyes, I'll sacrifice to your dear sense
And consecrate a fane to Confidence.

LYCUS.
But this you must at no hand tell your brother,
'Twill make him mad; for he that was before
So scourg'd but only with bare jealousy,   60
What would he be, if he should come to know it?

THARSALIO.
He would be less mad; for your only way
To clear his jealousy is to let him know it.

43. mind's] *Parrott;* windes *Q.*

---

46. *height of interjection*] "loud exclamations, with reference either to
Cynthia's laments for her husband, or her earlier emphatic protests against
a widow's second marriage" (Parrott).
57. *fane*] temple.

When knowledge comes, suspicion vanishes.
The sunbeams breaking forth swallow the mists.   65
But as for you, sir gallant, howsoever
Your banquet seems sweet in your liquorous palate,
It shall be sure to turn gall in your maw.
Thy hand a little, Lycus, here without.

LYCUS.

To what?

THARSALIO.   No booty serve you, sir soldado,   70
But my poor sister? Come, lend me thy shoulder;
I'll climb the cross. It will be such a cooler
To my venerean gentleman's hot liver,
When he shall find one of his crucified bodies
Stol'n down, and he to be forthwith made fast   75
In place thereof, for the sign
Of the lost sentinel. Come, glorify
Firm Confidence in great inconstancy.
And this believe (for all prov'd knowledge swears)
He that believes in error, never errs.   *Exeunt.* 80

The tomb opens, [disclosing] Lysander, Cynthia, Ero.

LYSANDER.

'Tis late; I must away.

CYNTHIA.   Not yet, sweet love.

LYSANDER.

Tempt not my stay, 'tis dangerous. The law is strict, and
not to be dispens'd with. If any sentinel be too late in's
watch, or that by his neglect one of the crucified bodies
should be stolen from the cross, his life buys it.   85

CYNTHIA.

A little stay will not endanger them.
The day's proclaimer has not yet given warning,
The cock yet has not beat his third alarm.

80.1 *disclosing*] *Parrott.*

67–68. *Your . . . maw*] Chapman's rendering of the proverb "What is
sweet (good) in the mouth (in taste), is oft sour (bitter) in the maw (belly,
at the heart)" (Tilley, M 1265).
88. *cock . . . alarm*] an hour before day.

LYSANDER.

What! Shall we ever dwell here amongst th' Antipodes?
Shall I not enjoy the honor of my fortune in public, sit in   90
Lysander's chair, reign in his wealth?

CYNTHIA.

Thou shalt, thou shalt. Though my love to thee
Hath prov'd thus sudden, and for haste leapt over
The complement of wooing,
Yet only for the world's opinion—   95

LYSANDER.

Mark that again.

CYNTHIA.

—I must maintain a form in parting hence.

LYSANDER.

Out upon't! Opinion, the blind goddess of fools, foe to the
virtuous, and only friend to undeserving persons, contemn
it. Thou know'st thou hast done virtuously. Thou hast   100
strangely sorrow'd for thy husband, follow'd him to death,
further thou could'st not; thou hast buried thyself quick—
[*Aside.*] O that 'twere true—spent more tears over his
carcass than would serve a whole city of saddest widows in
a plague time, besides sighings and swoonings not to be 105
credited.

CYNTHIA.

True, but those compliments might have their time, for
fashion sake.

LYSANDER.

Right, opinion and fashion. 'Sfoot, what call you time?
Th'ast wept these four whole days.   110

ERO.

Nay, by'rlady, almost five.

LYSANDER.

Look you there, near upon five whole days.

CYNTHIA.

Well, go and see; return, we'll go home.

94–95. *Shepherd; Q prints as one line.*   103. *Aside.* O . . . true—] *Parrott;*
                                             (O . . . true) *Q.*

94. *complement of wooing*] formality of courtship.

[Cynthia *and* Ero *close the tomb.*]

LYSANDER.

Hell be thy home! Huge monsters damn ye and your whole
creation! O ye gods, in the height of her mourning, in a   115
tomb, within sight of so many deaths, her husband's
believ'd body in her eye, he dead a few days before! This
mirror of nuptial chastity, this votress of widow-constancy, to
change her faith, exchange kisses, embraces, with a stranger,
and, but my shame withstood, to give the utmost earnest   120
of her love to an eightpenny sentinel; in effect, to prostitute
herself upon her husband's coffin! Lust, impiety, hell,
womanhood itself, add, if you can, one step to this!

Enter Captain *with two or three* Soldiers.

CAPTAIN.

One of the crucified bodies taken down!

LYSANDER [*aside*].

Enough. ·   *Slinks away.* 125

CAPTAIN.

And the sentinel not to be heard of?

I SOLDIER.

No, sir.

CAPTAIN.

Make out; haste, search about for him! Does none of you
know him, nor his name?

2 SOLDIER.

He's but a stranger here of some four days' standing, and   130
we never set eye on him, but at setting the watch.

CAPTAIN.

For whom serves he? You look well to your watch, masters.

I SOLDIER.

For Seigneur Stratio, and whence he is, 'tis ignorant to us.
We are not correspondent for any but our own places.

113.1.] *this edn.; no S.D. in Q.*   125. S.D. *aside*] *Parrott.*

113.1] I assume that all the action of the tomb sequences is played on
the inner stage, and that Cynthia and Ero remain within, merely opening
or closing the curtains as the action demands. Lysander then would speak
his next lines on the outer stage. Cf. *Q* stage directions for V.i.155.1;
V.i.300.1; V.i.417; V.i.529.1.

134. *correspondent*] answerable (*OED*).

CAPTAIN.

   Y'are eloquent. Abroad, I say, let me have him.   135

                                  Exeunt [Soldiers].

   This negligence will by the Governor be wholly cast on me;
he hereby will suggest to the Viceroy that the city guards are
very carelessly attended.

   He loves me not, I know, because of late
   I knew him but of mean condition;   140
   But now by Fortune's injudicious hand,
   Guided by bribing courtiers, he is rais'd
   To this high seat of honor.
   Nor blushes he to see himself advanc'd
   Over the heads of ten times higher worths,   145
   But takes it all, forsooth, to his merits,
   And looks (as all upstarts do) for most huge observance.
   Well, my mind must stoop to his high place,
   And learn within itself to sever him from that,
   And to adore Authority the Goddess,   150
   However borne by an unworthy beast;
   And let the beast's dull apprehension take
   The honor done to Isis, done to himself.
   I must sit fast and be sure to give no hold
   To these fault-hunting enemies.   *Exit.* 155

Tomb opens, and Lysander *within lies along;* Cynthia *and* Ero.

LYSANDER.

   Pray thee, disturb me not; put out the lights.

ERO.

   Faith, I'll take a nap again.

CYNTHIA.

   Thou shalt not rest before I be resolv'd
   What happy wind hath driven thee back to harbor!
   Was it my love?   160

LYSANDER.

   No.

135.1 Soldiers] *Parrott.*   139–145.] *Shepherd; prose in* Q.
138. carelessly] *Dodsley;* caresly Q.   146–155.] *Parrott; prose in* Q.

   150–153. *And to . . . himself*] In L'Estrange's translation of *Aesop* (no.
487, edn. of 1692) is a fable about an ass who, bearing a sacred image,
imagined himself to be reverenced (Parrott).

CYNTHIA.

Yet say so, sweet, that with the thought thereof
I may enjoy all that I wish in earth.

LYSANDER.

I am sought for. A crucified body is stol'n while
I loiter'd here, and I must die for't.   165

CYNTHIA.

Die! All the gods forbid! O this affright
Torments me ten parts more than the sad loss
Of my dear husband.

LYSANDER [*aside*].   Damnation! —I believe thee.

CYNTHIA.

Yet hear a woman's wit;
Take counsel of necessity and it.   170
I have a body here, which once I lov'd
And honor'd above all, but that time's past—

LYSANDER [*aside*].

It is; revenge it, heaven.

CYNTHIA.

—That shall supply at so extreme a need
The vacant gibbet.

LYSANDER.   Cancro! What, thy husband's body!   175

CYNTHIA.

What hurt is't, being dead, it save the living?

LYSANDER.

O heart, hold in; check thy rebellious motion!

CYNTHIA.

Vex not thyself, dear love, nor use delay.
Tempt not this danger; set thy hands to work.

LYSANDER.

I cannot do't; my heart will not permit   180
My hands to execute a second murder.
The truth is, I am he that slew thy husband.

162–163.] *Dodsley; prose in* Q.   *Parrott;* (Damnation) Q.
166–168.] *Reed; prose in* Q.   173. S.D. *aside.*] *Parrott.*
168. S.D.   *aside.*   Damnation!—]   174–175.] *Reed; prose in* Q.

---

175. *Cancro*] "the cancer take you," from the Italian (*OED*, citing this
passage).

CYNTHIA.

The gods forbid!

LYSANDER.

It was this hand that bath'd my reeking sword
In his life blood, while he cried out for mercy.   185
But I, remorseless, paunch'd him, cut his throat,
He with his last breath crying, "Cynthia."

CYNTHIA.

O thou hast told me news that cleaves my heart.
Would I had never seen thee, or heard sooner
This bloody story. Yet see, note my truth;   190
Yet I must love thee.

LYSANDER.   Out upon thee, monster!
Go, tell the Governor. Let me be brought
To die for that most famous villainy,
Not for this miching base transgression
Of truant negligence.

CYNTHIA.   I cannot do't.   195
Love must salve any murder. I'll be judge
Of thee, dear love, and these shall be thy pains,
Instead of iron, to suffer these soft chains.   [*Embracing him.*]

LYSANDER.

O, I am infinitely oblig'd.

CYNTHIA.

Arise, I say, thou saver of my life.   200
Do not with vain-affrighting conscience
Betray a life that is not thine, but mine.
Rise and preserve it.

LYSANDER.   Ha! Thy husband's body!
Hang't up, you say, instead of that that's stol'n,
Yet I his murderer; is that your meaning?   205

CYNTHIA.

It is, my love.

LYSANDER.   Thy love amazes me.
The point is yet how we shall get it thither.

191. thee, monster] *Reed;* the Mon-   195. truant] *Dodsley;* tenant Q.
ster Q.   198. S.D. *Embracing him*] *Parrott.*

186. *paunch'd*] pierce or rip the belly.
194. *miching*] sneaking, or hiding like a truant; cf. V.i.540.

Ha! Tie a halter about's neck and drag him to the gallows;
Shall I, my love?
CYNTHIA.   So you may do indeed.
Or if your own strength will not serve, we'll aid   210
Our hands to yours, and bear him to the place.
For heaven's love, come; the night goes off apace.
LYSANDER [aside].
All the infernal plagues dwell in thy soul!—
I'll fetch a crow of iron to break the coffin.
CYNTHIA.
Do, love; be speedy.
LYSANDER [aside].   As I wish thy damnation!   215

    Shut the tomb. [Lysander *comes forward.*]

O, I could tear myself into atoms! Off with this antic; the
shirt that Hercules wore for his wife was not more baneful.
[*Throwing off his armor.*]   Is't possible there should be such
a latitude in the sphere of this sex, to entertain such an
extension of mischief and not turn devil? What is a woman?   220
What are the worst when the best are so past naming? As
men like this, let them try their wives again. Put women to
the test; discover them; paint them, paint them ten parts
more than they do themselves, rather than look on them as
they are; their wits are but painted that dislike their   225
painting.
Thou foolish thirster after idle secrets

208–209.] *Collier; prose in* Q.	*Parrott.*
213. S.D. *aside*] *Parrott.*	227–228.] *Shepherd; prose in* Q.
215. S.D. *aside*] *Parrott.*	227–232.] *lineation as in Parrott;*
215.1. Lysander . . . *forward*]	*prose,* Thou . . . thee, *then verse* There
Parrott.	. . . enough./ As . . . receives,/ Or
218. S.D. *Throwing . . . armor*]	. . . leaves. Q.

216. *antic*] disguise.
227–232. *Thou . . . leaves*] *Copie* (l. 230) means "copious." Thus, briefly
paraphrased, the lines mean that Lysander has been assailed by copious ills,
which he feels are as numerous as the streams which flow into the Alizon
or as the leaves in the forest of Mt. Ida. "The Acheloüs was the largest
river in Greece, and its river-god, of the same name, was regarded as the
father of rivers. In a combat with Hercules one of the god's horns was torn
off by the hero, and this horn, according to Ovid, *Metamorphoses*, ix, 87–88,
was the horn of plenty. Lysander, with reference to the 'horn' which his

And ills abroad, look home, and store and choke thee;
There sticks an Acheloüs' horn of ill,
Copie enough;   230
As much as Alizon of streams receives,
Or lofty Ida shows of shady leaves.

Enter Tharsalio.

Who's that?

THARSALIO.

I wonder Lycus fails me. Nor can I hear what's become
of him. He would not, certain, ride to Dipolis to call my 235
brother back without my knowledge.

LYSANDER [*aside*].

My brother's voice; what makes he hereabouts so un-
timely? I'll slip him.   *Exiturus.*

THARSALIO.

Who goes there?

LYSANDER.

A friend.   240

THARSALIO.

Dear friend, let's know you. [*Recognizing* Lysander.] A
friend least look'd for but most welcome, and with many a
long look expected here. What, sir, unbooted? Have you
been long arriv'd?

LYSANDER.

Not long, some two hours before night.   245

THARSALIO.

Well, brother, y'have the most rare, admirable, unmatch-
able wife that ever suffer'd for the sin of a husband. I
cannot blame your confidence indeed now, 'tis built on such
infallible ground. Lycus, I think, be gone to call you to the
rescue of her life. Why she! O incomprehensible!   250

229. Acheloüs] *Dodsley;* Achelons   232. Ida] *Dodsley;* Ilea *Q.*
Q.   237. S.D. *aside*] *Parrott.*
229. ill] *conj. Deighton, adopted Par-*   241. S.D. *Recognizing* Lysander]
rott; all *Q.*   *Parrott.*

---

wife's infidelity has bestowed on him, speaks of it as an *Acheloüs'* horn, not
of good, but *of ill.* . . . The name *Alizon* [l. 231] is puzzling. No such river
is known in classical geography; but Chapman may perhaps have meant the
Halys, the largest river in Asia Minor; Homer (*Iliad*, II, 856) mentions a
people *Alizones* of this region. . . ." (Parrott).

LYSANDER.

    I have heard all related since my arrival. We'll meet
tomorrow.   [*Going.*]

THARSALIO.

    What haste, brother? But was it related with what untoler-
able pains I and my mistress, her other friends, matrons
and magistrates, labor'd her diversion from that course?   255

LYSANDER.

    Yes, yes.

THARSALIO.

    What streams of tears she pour'd out, what tresses of her
hair she tore and offer'd on your suppos'd hearse!

LYSANDER.

    I have heard all.

THARSALIO.

    But above all, how since that time, her eyes never harbor'd   260
wink of slumber these six days; no, nor tasted the least
dram of any sustenance!

LYSANDER.

    How, is that assur'd?

THARSALIO.

    Not a scruple!

LYSANDER.

    Are you sure there came no soldier to her, nor brought her   265
victuals?

THARSALIO.

    Soldier? What soldier?

LYSANDER.

    Why some soldier of the watch, that attends the executed
bodies. Well, brother, I am in haste; tomorrow shall supply
this night's defect of conference. Adieu.   *Exit* Lysander.   270

THARSALIO.

    A soldier? Of the watch? Bring her victuals? Go to, brother,
I have you in the wind. He's unharness'd of all his traveling
accouterments; I came directly from's house, no word of
him there; he knows the whole relation; he's passionate.
All collections speak he was the soldier. What should be the   275

252. S.D. *Going*] Parrott.

---

275. *collections*] inferences.

riddle of this, that he is stol'n hither into a soldier's disguise?
He should have stayed at Dipolis to receive news from us.
Whether he suspected our relation, or had not patience to
expect it; or whether that furious, frantic, capricious devil
Jealousy hath toss'd him hither on his horns, I cannot con- 280
jecture. But the case is clear; he's the soldier. Sister, look
to your fame, your chastity's uncover'd. Are they here
still? Here, believe it, both most woefully weeping over the
bottle.   *He knocks [on the tomb].*

ERO.

Who's there?   285

THARSALIO.

Tharsalio; open.

ERO.

Alas, sir, 'tis no boot to vex your sister and yourself. She is
desperate and will not hear persuasion; she's very weak.

THARSALIO [*aside*].

Here's a truebred chambermaid. —Alas, I am sorry for't;
I have brought her meat and Candian wine to strengthen 290
her.

ERO.

O, the very naming on't will drive her into a swoon. Good
sir, forbear.

THARSALIO.

Yet open, sweet, that I may bless mine eyes
With sight of her fair shrine,   295
And of thy sweetest self (her famous panderess);
Open, I say! Sister, you hear me well,
Paint not your tomb without; we know too well
What rotten carcasses are lodg'd within.
Open, I say.   300

    Ero opens, and he sees [Cynthia's] *head laid on the coffin, etc.*

Sister, I have brought you tidings to wake you out of this
sleeping mummery.

---

284. S.D. *on the tomb*] *this edn.*   300.1.] *Q prints S.D. as dialogue in*
289. S.D. *aside*] *this edn.*   *roman.*
294–299.] *Parrott; prose in Q.*   300.1. Cynthia's] *this edn.;* her *Q.*

---

290. *Candian wine*] wine from the neighborhood of Candia, in Crete.

ERO.

Alas, she's faint, and speech is painful to her.

THARSALIO.

Well said, frubber! Was there no soldier here lately?

ERO.

A soldier! When?   305

THARSALIO.

This night, last night, tother night, and I know not how
many nights and days.

CYNTHIA.

Who's there?

ERO.

Your brother, mistress, that asks if there were not a soldier
here.   310

CYNTHIA.

Here was no soldier.

ERO.

Yes, mistress, I think here was such a one, though you took
no heed of him.

THARSALIO.

Go to, sister! Did not you join kisses, embraces, and plight
indeed with him, the utmost pledge of nuptial love with him? 315
Deny't, deny't; but first hear me a short story. The soldier
was your disguis'd husband, dispute it not. That you see
yonder is but a shadow, an empty chest containing nothing
but air. Stand not to gaze at it, 'tis true. This was a project
of his own contriving to put your loyalty and constant vows 320
to the test. Y'are warn'd, be arm'd.   *Exit.*

ERO.

O fie o' these perils!

CYNTHIA.

O Ero, we are undone!

ERO.

Nay, you'd ne'er be warn'd. I ever wish'd you to withstand
the push of that soldier's pike, and not enter him too deep 325
into your bosom, but to keep sacred your widow's vows
made to Lysander.

---

304. *frubber*] "furbisher, burnisher, or polisher" (*OED*).
321. *Y'are ... arm'd*] proverbial (Tilley, H 54).

CYNTHIA.

Thou did'st, thou did'st.

ERO.

Now you may see th'event. Well, our safety lies in our
speed; he'll do us mischief if we prevent not his coming.   330
Let's to your mother's, and there call out your mightiest
friends to guard you from his fury. Let them begin the
quarrel with him for practicing this villainy on your sex to
entrap your frailties.

CYNTHIA.

Nay, I resolve to sit out one brunt more,   335
To try to what aim he'll enforce his project.
Were he some other man, unknown to me,
His violence might awe me;
But knowing him as I do, I fear him not.
Do thou but second me, thy strength and mine   340
Shall master his best force,
If he should prove outrageous.
Despair, they say, makes cowards turn courageous.
Shut up the tomb.   *Shut the tomb.*

Enter one of the Soldiers *sent out before to seek the* Sentinel.

1 SOLDIER.

All pains are lost in hunting out this soldier. His fear 345
(adding wings to his heels) outgoes us as far as the fresh
hare the tir'd hounds. Who goes there?

Enter Second Soldier *another way.*

2 SOLDIER.

A friend.

1 SOLDIER.

O, your success and mine touching this sentinel tells, I
suppose, one tale; he's far enough, I undertake, by this time. 350

2 SOLDIER.

I blame him not. The law's severe (though just) and
cannot be dispens'd.

335–344.] *Parrott; prose in Q.*   *closes* (though . . . dispens'd) *in paren.*
351. (though just)] *Collier; Q en-*

1 SOLDIER.

Why should the laws of Paphos with more rigor than other
city laws pursue offenders, that, not appeas'd with their
lives' forfeit, exact a justice of them after death? And if a 355
soldier in his watch, forsooth, lose one of the dead bodies,
he must die for't. It seems the State needed no soldiers when
that was made a law.

2 SOLDIER.

So we may chide the fire for burning us,
Or say the bee's not good because she stings.   360
'Tis not the body the law respects, but the soldier's neglect,
when the watch (the guard and safety of the city) is left
abandon'd to all hazards. But let him go, and tell me if your
news sort with mine for Lycus, apprehended, they say, about
Lysander's murder.   365

1 SOLDIER.

'Tis true; he's at the Captain's lodge under guard, and
'tis my charge in the morning to unclose the leaden coffin
and discover the body. The Captain will assay an old conclusion, often approv'd, that at the murderer's sight the
blood revives again and boils afresh, and every wound has 370
a condemning voice to cry out guilty 'gainst the murderer.

2 SOLDIER.

O world, if this be true! His dearest friend,
His bed companion, whom of all his friends
He cull'd out for his bosom!

1 SOLDIER.

Tush, man, in this topsy-turvy world, friendship and 375
bosom kindness are but made covers for mischief, means
to compass ill. Near-allied trust is but a bridge for treason.
The presumptions cry loud against him; his answers found
disjointed, cross-legg'd, tripping up one another. He names
a town whither he brought Lysander murder'd by moun- 380
taineers; that's false; some of the dwellers have been here,
and all disclaim it. Besides, the wounds he bears in show are
such as shrews closely give their husbands, that never bleed,
and find to be counterfeit.

359–360.] *this edn.; prose in Q*.   372–374.] *this edn.; prose in Q*.

2 SOLDIER.

O that jade falsehood is never sound of all,   385
But halts of one leg still.
Truth pace is all upright, sound everywhere,
And like a die, sets ever on a square.
And how is Lycus his bearing in this condition?

1 SOLDIER.

Faith (as the manner of such desperate offenders is till it 390
come to the point), careless and confident, laughing at all
that seem to pity him. But leave it to th'event. 'Night,
fellow soldier; you'll not meet me in the morning at the
tomb and lend me your hand to the unrigging of Lysander's
hearse?   395

2 SOLDIER.

I care not if I do, to view heaven's power in this unbottom'd
cellar.
Blood, though it sleep a time, yet never dies;
The gods on murderers fix revengeful eyes.   *Exeunt.*

[*Enter*] Lysander *solus with a crow of iron and a halter, which he lays
down, and puts on his disguise again.*

LYSANDER.

Come, my borrow'd disguise, let me once more   400
Be reconcil'd to thee, my trustiest friend.
Thou that in truest shape hast let me see
That which my truer self hath hid from me,
Help me to take revenge on a disguise
Ten times more false and counterfeit than thou.   405
Thou, false in show, hast been most true to me;
The seeming true hath prov'd more false than thee.
Assist me to behold this act of lust;
Note, with a scene of strange impiety,
Her husband's murder'd corse! O more than horror!   410
I'll not believe't untried. If she but lift
A hand to act it, by the Fates her brains fly out;

385–386.] *Shepherd; prose in Q.*
387.] *Dodsley; prose in Q.*
395. hearse?] *Dodsley;* herse. *Q.*
399.1. *Enter*] *this edn.*

400. S.P. LYSANDER] *Dodsley; not in
Q.*
407. thee] *conj. Gilchrist in Collier edn.,
adopted Parrott;* her *Q.*

–97–

Since she has madded me, let her beware my horns;
For though by goring her no hope be shown
To cure myself, yet I'll not bleed alone.   *He knocks.*   415

ERO.

The soldier; open.   *She opens, and he enters.*
See, sweet, here are the engines that must do't,
Which, with much fear of my discovery,
I have at last procur'd.   420
Shall we about this work? I fear the morn
Will overtake's; my stay hath been prolong'd
With hunting obscure nooks for these employments.
The night prepares a way. Come, art resolv'd?

CYNTHIA.

Ay, you shall find me constant.   425

LYSANDER.

Ay, so I have; most prodigiously constant.
Here's a rare halter to hug him with.

ERO.

Better you and I join our hands and bear him thither; you
take his head.

CYNTHIA.

Ay, for that was always heavier than's whole body besides. 430

LYSANDER [*aside*].

You can tell best that loaded it.

ERO.

I'll be at the feet; I am able to bear against you, I warrant
you.

LYSANDER.

Hast thou prepar'd weak nature to digest
A sight so much distasteful? Hast sear'd thy heart   435
It bleed not at the bloody spectacle?
Hast arm'd thy fearful eyes against th' affront
Of such a direful object,

---

424. prepares a way] *Reed;* pre-   431. S.D. *aside*] *Parrott.*
pares away *Q.*   436. It] *Dodsley;* I *Q.*

423. *employments*] implements (*OED*).

Thy murder'd husband ghastly staring on thee,
His wounds gaping to affright thee, his body soil'd with gore? 440
'Fore heaven, my heart shrugs at it.

CYNTHIA.   So does not mine!
Love's resolute, and stands not to consult
With petty terror, but in full career
Runs blindfold through an army of misdoubts
And interposing fears; perhaps I'll weep   445
Or so, make a forc'd face, and laugh again.

LYSANDER.
O most valiant love!
I was thinking with myself as I came,
How if this break to light, his body known
(As many notes might make it), would it not fix   450
Upon thy fame an unremoved brand
Of shame and hate? They that in former times
Ador'd thy virtue, would they not abhor
Thy loathest memory?

CYNTHIA.
All this I know, but yet my love to thee   455
Swallows all this, or whatsoever doubts
Can come against it.
Shame's but a feather balanc'd with thy love.

LYSANDER.
Neither fear nor shame? You are steel to th' proof.
[*Aside.*]   But I shall iron you. —Come then; let's to work. 460
Alas, poor corpse, how many martyrdoms
Must thou endure, mangl'd by me a villain,
And now expos'd to foul shame of the gibbet!
'Fore piety, there is somewhat in me strives
Against the deed; my very arm relents   465
To strike a stroke so inhuman

439–441.] *Parrott;* Thy . . . thee,/   . . . it. *Q.*
His . . . with/ Gore . . . it *Q.*   459.] *Reed;* Neither . . . th'/ Proofe
448–449.] *Collier;* I . . . this/ Brake   *Q.*
. . . knowne *Q.*   460. *Aside* . . . you. —] *Parrott;* (but
455–457.] *Reed;* All . . . know/ But   . . . you) *Q.*
. . . thee/ Swallowes . . . doubts/ Can

460. *iron you*] catch you.

To wound a hallow'd hearse! Suppose 'twere mine,
Would not my ghost start up and fly upon thee?

CYNTHIA.

No, I'd mall it down again with this!   *She snatches up the crow.*

LYSANDER.

How now?   *He catches at her throat.*   470

CYNTHIA.

Nay, then I'll assay my strength; a soldier and afraid of a
dead man? A soft-roed milksop! Come, I'll do't myself.

LYSANDER.

And I look on? Give me the iron.

CYNTHIA.

No, I'll not lose the glory on't. This hand, *etc.*

LYSANDER.

Pray thee, sweet, let it not be said the savage act was thine;   475
deliver me the engine.

CYNTHIA.

Content yourself, 'tis in a fitter hand.

LYSANDER.

Wilt thou first? Art not thou the most—

CYNTHIA.

Ill-destin'd wife of a transform'd monster,
Who to assure himself of what he knew,   480
Hath lost the shape of man!

LYSANDER.   Ha! Cross-capers?

CYNTHIA.

Poor soldier's case; do not we know you, sir?
But I have given thee what thou cam'st to seek.
Go, satyr, run affrighted with the noise
Of that harsh-sounding horn thyself hast blown.   485
Farewell; I leave thee there my husband's corpse;
Make much of that.   *Exit cum* Ero.

LYSANDER.   What have I done?
O let me lie and grieve, and speak no more.   [*Tomb closes.*]

487–488.] *Parrott; prose in Q.*   488. S.D. *Tomb closes*] *Parrott.*

---

472. *soft-roed*] "soft roe" is the "milt or sperm of a male fish" (*OED*).
481. *Cross-capers*] "unexpected start, which *crosses* another's plans"
(Parrott).

[*Enter*] Captain, Lycus *with a guard of three or four* Soldiers.

CAPTAIN.

    Bring him away. You must have patience, sir; if you can
say ought to quit you of those presumptions that lie heavy 490
on you, you shall be heard. If not, 'tis not your braves nor
your affecting looks can carry it. We must acquit our duties.

LYCUS.

    Y'are captain o'th' watch, sir?

CAPTAIN.

    You take me right.

LYCUS.

    So were you best do me. See your presumptions be strong, 495
or be assured that shall prove a dear presumption, to brand
me with the murder of my friend. But you have been
suborn'd by some close villain to defame me.

CAPTAIN.

    'Twill not be so put off, friend Lycus. I could wish your
soul as free from taint of this foul fact, as mine from any such 500
unworthy practice.

LYCUS.

    Conduct me to the Governor himself, to confront before
him your shallow accusations.

CAPTAIN.

    First, sir, I'll bear you to Lysander's tomb to confront the
murder'd body, and see what evidence the wounds will yield 505
against you.

LYCUS.

    Y'are wise, Captain. But if the body should chance not to
speak; if the wounds should be tongue-tied, Captain;
where's then your evidence, Captain? Will you not be
laugh'd at for an officious captain?   510

CAPTAIN.

    Y'are gallant, sir.

LYCUS.

    Your Captainship commands my service no further.

CAPTAIN.

    Well, sir, perhaps I may, if this conclusion take not; we'll

488.1. *Enter*] *Parrott.*

---

491. *braves*] boastful or threatening behavior.

try what operation lies in torture, to pull confession from
you.   515

LYCUS.

Say you so, Captain? But hark you, Captain, might it not
concur with the quality of your office, ere this matter grow
to the height of a more threatening danger, to wink a little
at a by-slip, or so?

CAPTAIN.

How's that?   520

LYCUS.

To send a man abroad under guard of one of your silliest
shack-rags, that he may beat the knave, and run's way. I
mean this on good terms, Captain; I'll be thankful.

CAPTAIN.

I'll think on't hereafter. Meantime, I have other employment for you.   525

LYCUS.

Your place is worthily replenish'd, Captain. My duty, sir.
Hark, Captain, there's a mutiny in your army; I'll go raise
the Governor.   *Exiturus.*

CAPTAIN.

No haste, sir; he'll soon be here without your summons.

Soldiers *thrust up* Lysander *from the tomb.*

I SOLDIER.

Bring forth the Knight o'th' Tomb. Have we met with you,   530
sir?

LYSANDER.

Pray thee, soldier, use thine office with better temper.

2 SOLDIER.

Come, convey him to the Lord Governor.

LYSANDER.

First afore the Captain, sir. [*Aside.*] Have the heavens
nought else to do, but to stand still and turn all their malig- 535
nant aspects upon one man?

534. S.P. LYSANDER] *conj. Collier,*   First afore . . ..
accepted Shepherd; continuation of 2nd   534. S.D. *Aside*] *Parrott.*
Soldier's speech Q, i.e., Gouernour,/

2 SOLDIER.

Captain, here's the sentinel we sought for; he's some new-press'd soldier, for none of us know him.

CAPTAIN.

Where found you him?

I SOLDIER.

My truant was mich'd, sir, into a blind corner of the tomb. 540

CAPTAIN.

Well said, guard him safe. But for the corpse?

I SOLDIER.

For the corpse, sir? Bare misprision, there's no body, nothing. A mere blandation, a *deceptio visus*, unless this soldier for hunger have eat up Lysander's body.

LYCUS.

Why, I could have told you this before, Captain. The body 545 was borne away piecemeal by devout ladies of Venus' order, for the man died one of Venus' martyrs. And yet I heard since 'twas seen whole o'th' other side the downs upon a colestaff betwixt two huntsmen, to feed their dogs withal; which was a miracle, Captain.   550

CAPTAIN.

Mischief in this act hath a deep bottom and requires more time to sound it. But you, sir, it seems, are a soldier of the newest stamp. Know you what 'tis to forsake your stand? There's one of the bodies in your charge stol'n away; how answer you that? See, here comes the Governor.   555

Enter a Guard, *bare, after the* Governor. Tharsalio, Argus, *Clinias,*
before Eudora; Cynthia, *Laodice, Sthenia, Ianthe, Ero, etc.*

GUARD.

Stand aside there!

CAPTAIN [*aside*].

Room for a strange Governor. The perfect draught of a most brainless, imperious upstart. O desert! Where wert thou when this wooden dagger was gilded over with the title of Governor?   560

541. But] *Dodsley;* bur *Q.*   557. S.D. *aside*] *Collier.*

---

543. *blandation*] illusion (*OED*).

549. *colestaff*] a stout stick thrust through the handles of a "cowl" or tub, and carried on the shoulders of two bearers.

GUARD.

Peace, masters, hear my lord.

THARSALIO.

All wisdom be silent; now speaks authority.

GOVERNOR.

I am come in person to discharge justice.

THARSALIO.

Of his office.

GOVERNOR.

The cause you shall know hereafter, and it is this. A villain, 565
whose very sight I abhor— where is he? Let me see him.

CAPTAIN.

Is't Lycus you mean, my lord?

GOVERNOR.

Go to, sirrah, y'are too malapert; I have heard of your
sentinel's escape. Look to't.

CAPTAIN.

My lord, this is the sentinel you speak of.   570

GOVERNOR.

How now, sir? What time o'day is't?

ARGUS.

I cannot show you precisely, an't please your honor.

GOVERNOR.

What! Shall we have replications, rejoinders?

THARSALIO [aside].

Such a creature fool is, when he bestrides the back of
authority.   575

GOVERNOR.

Sirrah, stand you forth. It is supposed thou hast com-
mitted a most inconvenient murder upon the body of
Lysander.

LYCUS.

My good lord, I have not.

GOVERNOR.

Peace, varlet. Dost chop with me? I say it is imagined thou 580
hast murder'd Lysander. How it will be prov'd, I know not.

574. S.D. aside] Parrott.

---

573. replications, rejoinders] the two words are synonymous.
580. chop] bandy words; a shortened form of "chop logic."

Thou shalt therefore presently be had to execution, as justice
in such cases requireth. Soldiers, take him away; bring forth
the sentinel.

LYCUS.

Your lordship will first let my defense be heard.   585

GOVERNOR.

Sirrah, I'll no fending nor proving. For my part, I am
satisfied it is so; that's enough for thee. I had ever a
sympathy in my mind against him. Let him be had away.

THARSALIO [aside].

A most excellent apprehension. He's able, ye see, to judge of
a cause at first sight, and hear but two parties. Here's a   590
second Solon.

EUDORA.

Hear him, my lord. Presumptions oftentimes
(Though likely grounded) reach not to the truth,
And truth is oft abus'd by likelihood.
Let him be heard, my lord.   595

GOVERNOR.

Madam, content yourself. I will do justice; I will not hear
him. Your late lord was my honorable predecessor, but
your ladyship must pardon me. In matters of justice I am
blind.

THARSALIO [aside].

That's true.   600

GOVERNOR.

I know no persons. If a court favorite write to me in a
case of justice, I will pocket his letter and proceed. If a
suitor in a case of justice thrusts a bribe into my hand, I
will pocket his bribe and proceed. Therefore, madam, set
your heart at rest. I am seated in the throne of justice, and 605
I will do justice; I will not hear him.

EUDORA.

Not hear him, my lord?

GOVERNOR.

No, my lady, and moreover put you in mind in whose

588. Let . . . away] *Reed; Q prints as*   589. S.D. *aside*] *Parrott.*
separate line.   600. S.D. *aside*] *Parrott.*

586. *I'll . . . proving*] i.e., I'll hear no defenses nor proofs.

presence you stand. If you parrot to me long, go to.

THARSALIO [*aside*].

Nay, the Vice must snap his authority at all he meets; 610
how shall't else be known what part he plays?

GOVERNOR.

Your husband was a noble gentleman, but, alas, he came
short; he was no statesman. He has left a foul city behind
him.

THARSALIO [*aside*].

Ay, and I can tell you 'twill trouble his lordship and all his 615
honorable assistants of scavengers to sweep it clean.

GOVERNOR.

It's full of vices, and great ones too.

THARSALIO [*aside*].

And thou none of the meanest.

GOVERNOR.

But I'll turn all topsy-turvy, and set up a new discipline
amongst you. I'll cut off all perish'd members— 620

THARSALIO [*aside*].

That's the surgeon's office.

GOVERNOR.

—Cast out these rotten stinking carcasses for infecting the
whole city.

ARGUS.

Rotten they may be, but their wenches use to pepper
them, and their surgeons to parboil them, and that pre- 625
serves them from stinking, an't please your honor.

GOVERNOR.

Peace, sirrah, peace; and yet 'tis well said, too. A good
pregnant fellow, i'faith. But to proceed. I will spew
drunkenness out o'th' city.

THARSALIO [*aside*].

Into th' country. 630

---

609. parrot] *Dodsley;* Parrat *Q*.   618. S.D. *aside*] *Parrott.*
610. S.D. *aside*] *Parrott.*   621. S.D. *aside*] *Parrott.*
615. S.D. *aside*] *Parrott.*   630. S.D. *aside*] *Parrott.*

---

625. *parboil*] reference to the surgeon's tub (Parrott).
628. *pregnant*] imaginative, resourceful.

GOVERNOR.

Shifters shall cheat and starve, and no man shall do good
but where there is no need. Braggarts shall live at the head,
and the tumult that haunt taverns. Asses shall bear good
qualities, and wise men shall use them. I will whip lechery
out o'th' city; there shall be no more cuckolds. They that 635
heretofore were errant cornutos, shall now be honest shopkeepers, and justice shall take place. I will hunt jealousy
out of my dominion.

THARSALIO [aside].

Do hear, brother?

GOVERNOR.

It shall be the only note of love to the husband, to love the 640
wife; and none shall be more kindly welcome to him than he
that cuckolds him.

THARSALIO [aside].

Believe it, a wholesome reformation.

GOVERNOR.

I'll have no more beggars. Fools shall have wealth, and the
learned shall live by their wits. I'll have no more bank- 645
routs. They that owe money shall pay it at their best leisure,
and the rest shall make a virtue of imprisonment, and their
wives shall help to pay their debts. I'll have all young widows
spaded for marrying again. For the old and wither'd, they
shall be confiscate to unthrifty gallants and decay'd knights. 650
If they be poor, they shall be burnt to make soap-ashes, or
given to Surgeon's Hall to be stamp'd to salve for the
French measles. To conclude, I will cart pride out o'th'
town.

ARGUS.

An't please your honor, Pride, an't be ne'er so beggarly, 655
will look for a coach.

GOVERNOR.

Well said, o' mine honor. A good significant fellow, i'faith.
What is he? He talks much. Does he follow your ladyship?

639. S.D. aside] Parrott.   643. S.D. aside] Parrott.

636. *cornutos*] cuckolds.
653. *French measles*] an allusion to venereal disease, often connected with
France.

ARGUS.

No, an't please your honor, I go before her.

GOVERNOR.

A good undertaking presence, a well-promising forehead. 660
Your gentleman usher, madam?

EUDORA.

Yours, if you please, my lord.

GOVERNOR.

Born i'th' city?

ARGUS.

Ay, an't please your honor, but begot i'th' court.

GOVERNOR.

Tressel-legg'd?   665

ARGUS.

Ay, an't please your honor.

GOVERNOR.

The better; it bears a breadth, makes room o'both sides.
Might I not see his pace?

ARGUS.

Yes, an't please your honor.   Argus *stalks*.

GOVERNOR.

'Tis well, 'tis very well. Give me thy hand. Madam, I will 670
accept this property at your hand, and will wear it thread-
bare for your sake. Fall in there, sirrah. And for the matter
of Lycus, madam, I must tell you, you are shallow. There's
a state point in't! Hark you. The Viceroy has given him,
and we must uphold correspondence; he must walk. Say one 675
man goes wrongfully out o'th' world, there are hundreds to
one come wrongfully into th' world.

EUDORA.

Your lordship will give me but a word in private?

[*Whispers to the* Governor.]

669. S.D. Argus *stalks*] *Dodsley; Q*   678.1. *Whispers . . .* Governor]
prints on preceding line.   *Parrott.*

665. *Tressel-legg'd*] legs set wide apart, as in the support for a bridge or a
stool.
667. *bears a breadth*] In a note to *Monsieur D'Olive* (IV.ii.103), Parrott
explains the phrase as meaning to "carry affairs of importance."
668. *pace*] A gentleman usher was expected to have a special "pace" as
he walked before his master or mistress; the "pace" of a gentleman usher
is referred to in many plays of the period.

THARSALIO.

Come, brother, we know you well. What means this habit?
Why stayed you not at Dipolis as you resolv'd, to take   680
advertisement for us of your wife's bearing?

LYSANDER.

O brother, this jealous frenzy has borne me headlong to
ruin.

THARSALIO.

Go to, be comforted. Uncase yourself and discharge your
friend.   685

GOVERNOR.

Is that Lysander, say you? And is all his story true? By'rlady,
madam, this jealousy will cost him dear. He undertook the
person of a soldier, and, as a soldier, must have justice.
Madam, his Altitude in this case cannot dispense. Lycus,
this soldier hath acquitted you.   690

THARSALIO.

And that acquital I'll for him requite; the body lost is by this
time restor'd to his place.

I SOLDIER.

It is, my lord.

THARSALIO.

These are State points, in which your lordship's time
Has not yet train'd your lordship; please your lordship   695
To grace a nuptial we have now in hand

> Hylus *and* Laodice *stand together.*

'Twixt this young lady and this gentleman.
Your lordship there shall hear the ample story.
And how the ass wrapp'd in a lion's skin
Fearfully roar'd; but his large ears appear'd   700
And made him laugh'd at, that before was fear'd.

GOVERNOR.

I'll go with you. For my part, I am at a non-plus.

> Eudora *whispers with* Cynthia.

693. S.P. 1] *this edn.*   695–696.] *Shepherd; prose in* Q.

680–681. *take . . . us*] be advised by us.
699–701. *And how . . .fear'd*] The fable of the ass and the skin of the lion
was printed in 1484 by Caxton in *Fab. Avian* 4, and by the time of Chapman
had become proverbial (Tilley, A 351).
702. *at a non-plus*] perplexed, puzzled.

THARSALIO.

    Come, brother, thank the Countess. She hath sweat
To make your peace. Sister, give me your hand.
So, brother, let your lips compound the strife,   705
And think you have the only constant wife.   *Exeunt.*

703–704.] *Collier; prose in Q.*   706. S.D. *Exeunt*] Q *(corr.)*; *not in* Q
                                                    (uncorr.).

Appendix

Chronology

Approximate years are indicated by *, occurrences in doubt by (?).

1558
Accession of Queen Elizabeth I.
Robert Greene born.
Thomas Kyd born.
1560

George Chapman born in Hitchin in Hertfordshire.*

1561
Francis Bacon born.
1564
Shakespeare born.
Christopher Marlowe born.
1570
Thomas Heywood born.*
1572
Thomas Dekker born.*
John Donne born.
Massacre of St. Bartholomew's Day.
1573
Ben Jonson born.*
1574

"Sent to the University" (probably Oxford, and later to Cambridge) "where he was observed to be most excellent in the Latin and Greek tongues" but "took no degree there" (Wood).*

1576
The Theatre, the first permanent

public theater in London, established by James Burbage.

John Marston born.

1577

The Cutain theater opened.

Holinshed's *Chronicles of England, Scotland and Ireland*.

Drake begins circumnavigation of the earth; completed 1580.

1578

John Lyly's *Euphues: The Anatomy of Wit*.

1579

John Fletcher born.

Sir Thomas North's translation of Plutarch's *Lives*.

1580

Thomas Middleton born.

1583

Philip Massinger born.

1584

Francis Beaumont born.*

1586

Death of Sir Philip Sidney.

John Ford born.

1587

The Rose theater opened by Henslowe.

Marlowe's *TAMBURLAINE*, Part I.*

Execution of Mary, Queen of Scots.

Drake raids Cadiz.

1588

Defeat of the Spanish Armada.

Marlowe's *TAMBURLAINE*, Part II.*

1589

Greene's *FRIAR BACON AND FRIAR BUNGAY*.*

Marlowe's *THE JEW OF MALTA*.*

Kyd's *THE SPANISH TRAGEDY.**

1590
Spenser's *Faerie Queene* (Books I–III) published.
Sidney's *Arcadia* published.
Shakespeare's *HENRY VI*, Parts I–III,* *TITUS ANDRONICUS.**

1591
Shakespeare's *RICHARD III.** | In Low Countries as member of English Expeditionary Force (?).

1592
Marlowe's *DOCTOR FAUSTUS** and *EDWARD II.**
Shakespeare's *TAMING OF THE SHREW** and *THE COMEDY OF ERRORS.**
Death of Greene.

1593
Shakespeare's *LOVE'S LABOUR'S LOST;** *Venus and Adonis* published. | Associating with Raleigh, Roydon, Marlowe, and Harriot in the "School of Night."*
Death of Marlowe.
Theaters closed on account of plague.

1594
Shakespeare's *TWO GENTLE-MEN OF VERONA;** *The Rape of Lucrece* published. | *The Shadow of the Night* (*Hymnus in Noctem* and *Hymnus in Cynthiam*).
Shakespeare's company becomes Lord Chamberlain's Men.
Death of Kyd.

1595
The Swan theater built. | *Ovid's Banquet of Sense, A Coronet for His Mistress Philosophy, and His Amorous Zodiac.*
Sidney's *Defense of Poesy* published.
Shakespeare's *ROMEO AND JULIET,** *A MIDSUMMER NIGHT'S DREAM,** *RICHARD II.**
Raleigh's first expedition to Guiana.

1596
Spenser's *Faerie Queene* (Books IV–VI) published. | Chapman writing for the Admiral's company.*

Shakespeare's *MERCHANT OF VENICE,* KING JOHN.*
James Shirley born.

1597
Bacon's *Essays* (first edition).
Shakespeare's *HENRY IV*, Part I.*

1598
Demolition of The Theatre.
Shakespeare's *MUCH ADO ABOUT NOTHING,* HENRY IV*, Part II.* Jonson's *EVERY MAN IN HIS HUMOR* (first version).

1599
The Paul's Boys reopen their theater.
The Globe theater opened.
Shakespeare's *AS YOU LIKE IT,* HENRY V, JULIUS CAESAR.*
Dekker's *THE SHOEMAKERS' HOLIDAY.*
Marston's *ANTONIO AND MELLIDA,* Parts I and II.
Death of Spenser.

1600
Shakespeare's *TWELFTH NIGHT.*
The Fortune theater built by Alleyn.
The Children of the Chapel begin to play at the Blackfriars.

1601
Shakespeare's *HAMLET,* MERRY VIVES OF WINDSOR.*
Insurrection and execution of the Earl of Essex.
Jonson's *POETASTER.*

1602
Shakespeare's *TROILUS AND CRESSIDA.*

THE BLIND BEGGAR OF ALEXANDRIA (printed 1598).
De Guiana.

AN HUMOROUS DAY'S MIRTH (printed 1599), a prototype of the comedy of humors.

Mentioned by Meres in *Palladis Tamia* as one of the best writers of comedy and tragedy.
Completes *Hero and Leander; Seven Books of the Iliads* (tr.); *Achilles Shield* (tr.).

Begins writing for the recently revived children companies, Paul's Boys and the Children of the Chapel.

THE CONSPIRACY AND TRAGEDY OF CHARLES, DUKE OF BYRON (printed 1608); *THE GENTLEMAN USHER* (printed 1606); *SIR GILES GOOSE-CAP* (?)* (printed 1606).

1603

Death of Queen Elizabeth I; accession of James VI of Scotland as James I. Florio's translation of Montaigne's *Essays* published. Shakespeare's *ALL'S WELL THAT ENDS WELL.** Heywood's *A WOMAN KILLED WITH KINDNESS.* Marston's *THE MALCONTENT.** Shakespeare's company becomes the King's Men.

Becomes protégé of Prince Henry, who appoints him his "sewer in ordinary" in 1604.

1604

Shakespeare's *MEASURE FOR MEASURE,** *OTHELLO.** Marston's *THE FAWN.**

ALL FOOLS* (printed 1605); *MONSIEUR D'OLIVE** (printed 1606); *BUSSY D'AMBOIS** (printed 1607).

1605

Shakespeare's *KING LEAR.** Marston's *THE DUTCH COURTEZAN.** Bacon's *Advancement of Learning* published. The Gunpowder Plot.

THE WIDOW'S TEARS* (printed 1612); *THE TRAGEDY OF CAESAR AND POMPEY** (printed 1631). *EASTWARD HO*, in collaboration with Jonson and Marston (printed 1605); Chapman and Jonson imprisoned because of alleged derogatory allusions to King James.

1606

Shakespeare's *MACBETH.** Jonson's *VOLPONE.** Tourneur's *REVENGER'S TRAGEDY.** The Red Bull theater built. Death of John Lyly.

1607

Shakespeare's *ANTONY AND CLEOPATRA.** Beaumont's *KNIGHT OF THE BURNING PESTLE.** Settlement of Jamestown, Virginia.

1608

Shakespeare's *CORIOLANUS,* TIMON OF ATHENS,* PERICLES.**
Dekker's *Gull's Hornbook* published.
Richard Burbage leases Blackfriars Theatre for King's company.
John Milton born.

A spring performance of the *BYRON* plays with an indecorous presentation on the stage of the living French Queen results in vehement protests of the French Ambassador and to wholesale excisions in the printed text.

1609

Shakespeare's *CYMBELINE;**
Sonnets published.
Jonson's *EPICOENE.*

Euthymiae Raptus, or the Tears of Peace; Twelve Books of the Iliads (tr). *MAY DAY** (printed 1611).

1610

Jonson's *ALCHEMIST.*
Richard Crashaw born.

BUSSY D'AMBOIS revised* (printed 1641); *REVENGE OF BUSSY D'AMBOIS** (printed 1613).

1611

Authorized (King James) Version of the Bible published.
Shakespeare's *THE WINTER'S TALE,* THE TEMPEST.**
Beaumont and Fletcher's *A KING AND NO KING.*
Middleton's *A CHASTE MAID IN CHEAPSIDE.**
Tourneur's *ATHEIST'S TRAGEDY.**

The complete *Iliads* (tr.).

1612

Webster's *THE WHITE DEVIL.**

Petrarch's Seven Penitential Psalms [tr.] *. . . and a Hymn to Christ upon the Cross; An Epicede, or Funeral Song* (on the death on November 6 of Prince Henry).

1613

The Globe theater burned.
Shakespeare's *HENRY VIII* (with Fletcher).
Webster's *THE DUCHESS OF MALFI.**
Sir Thomas Overbury murdered.

THE MASQUE OF THE MIDDLE TEMPLE AND LINCOLN'S INN (set designed by Inigo Jones), performed on February 15 as part of the entertainment celebrating the marriage of Princess Elizabeth to Palsgrave, the Elector Palatine (printed 1613).

1614
The Globe theater rebuilt.
The Hope Theatre built.
Jonson's *BARTHOLOMEW FAIR.*

Eugenia; Andromeda Liberata, or The Nuptials of Perseus and Andromeda; Justification of . . . Andromeda Liberata.

1615

The complete *Odysseys* (tr.).

1616
Publication of Folio edition of Jonson's *Works.*
Death of Shakespeare.
Death of Beaumont.

The Whole Works of Homer (tr.); *Divine Poem of Musaeus* (tr.).

1618
Outbreak of Thirty Years War.
Execution of Raleigh.

Georgics of Hesiod (tr.).

1620
Settlement of Plymouth, Massachusetts.

1621
Middleton's *WOMEN BEWARE WOMEN.**
Robert Burton's *Anatomy of Melancholy* published.
Andrew Marvell born.

*THE TRAGEDY OF CHABOT, ADMIRAL OF FRANCE** (written 1621–1624, printed 1639).

1622
Middleton and Rowley's *THE CHANGELING.**
Henry Vaughan born.

Pro Vere, Autumni Lachrymae.

1623
Publication of Folio edition of Shakespeare's *COMEDIES, HISTORIES, AND TRAGEDIES.*

*An Invective . . . against Mr. Ben Jonson.**

1624

Crown of All Homer's Works (tr.).**

1625
Death of King James I; accession of Charles I.
Death of Fletcher.

1626
Death of Tourneur.
Death of Bacon.

1627
Death of Middleton.

1628
Ford's *THE LOVER'S MELAN-
CHOLY.*
Petition of Right.
Buckingham assassinated.

1629

Fifth Satire of Juvenal (tr.).

1631
Shirley's *THE TRAITOR.*
Death of Donne.
John Dryden born.

1632
Massinger's *THE CITY MADAM.**

1633
Donne's *Poems* published.
Death of George Herbert.

1634
Death of Marston, Webster.*
Publication of *THE TWO NOBLE
KINSMEN,* with title-page attri-
bution to Shakespeare and Fletcher.
Milton's *Comus.*

Chapman dies on May 12; buried
in the parish of St. Giles-in-the
Fields, where Inigo Jones erects a
monument to his memory.

1635
Sir Thomas Brown's *Religio Medici.*

1637
Death of Jonson.

1639
First Bishops' War.
Death of Carew.*

1640
Short Parliament.
Long Parliament impeaches Laud.
Death of Massinger, Burton.

1641
Irish rebel.
Death of Heywood.

Revision of *BUSSY D'AMBOIS*
published.

1642
Charles I leaves London; Civil War
breaks out.
Shirley's *COURT SECRET.*
All theaters closed by Act of
Parliament.

1643
Parliament swears to the Solemn
League and Covenant.

1645
Ordinance for New Model Army
enacted.

1646
End of First Civil War.

1647
Army occupies London.
Charles I forms alliance with Scots.
Publication of Folio edition of
Beaumont and Fletcher's *COM-
EDIES AND TRAGEDIES.*